BUSINESS
LEADERSHIP
AND INCLUSION
AND ACCESSIBILITY

MAXIMIZE YOUR BUSINESS'S POTENTIAL
WITH STRATEGIC LEADERSHIP AND
INCLUSION AND ACCESSIBILITY

JASON MILLER

FOREWORD BY DR. KIRK ADAMS

CHRIS O'BYRNE, PATRICIA BARONOWSKI-SCHNEIDER,
IRA BOWMAN, DR. JULIE DUCHARME, LYNN HOERAUF,
RYAN AND BRIANNA JACKSON, MIKE JACKSON,
MICHAEL MARKIEWICZ, JESSICA POWERS,
DR. BRUCE RIPPEE, LUBA SAKHARUK, DAVID WOLF

ISBN: 978-1-957217-27-7 (hardback)

ISBN: 978-1-957217-28-4 (paperback)

ISBN: 978-1-957217-29-1 (ebook)

CONTENTS

FOREWORD

BY
DR. KIRK ADAMS

SUPERCHARGE BOTTOM LINE BUSINESS RESULTS WITH DISABILITY INCLUSION

Dr. Kirk Adams is an expert in disability inclusion, having served as the former president and CEO of the American Foundation for the Blind. His extensive experience in the field has led him to work with government agencies, corporations, and nonprofit organizations to develop policies and practices that promote disability inclusion. Dr. Adams holds a PhD in Leadership and Change, and his dissertation, "Journeys Through Rough Country," focused on the experiences of people with disabilities navigating barriers to inclusion in society. He has also been recognized for his contributions to the field, with numerous awards and honors. Dr. Adams' firsthand experience with visual impairment fuels his passion for disability inclusion, and he strives toward a more equitable and inclusive society for all.

Disability inclusion is a sound business decision that can be framed through Amartya Sen's capabilities approach. This approach emphasizes creating a society where everyone can live a fulfilling life rather than focusing on economic growth. Disability inclusion is an essential element of this approach, as it enables people with disabilities to participate fully in society and enjoy the same opportunities as others. According to the Accenture report on the business case for disability inclusion, companies that intentionally include people with disabilities in their workforce can expect improved bottom-line business results. Specifically, companies with strong disability policies and practices are 28% more likely to outperform their peers financially.

Moreover, disability-inclusive businesses can tap into a larger consumer market, as people with disabilities comprise a significant portion of the consumer population. The DuPont longitudinal study provides further evidence of the advantages of disability inclusion. The study demonstrated that employees with disabilities had lower turnover rates, higher attendance rates, and fewer workplace accidents than their non-disabled peers, contributing to a more productive workforce and ultimately improving the company's bottom line. Randy Lewis's experience with Walgreens in Anderson, SC, provides a concrete example of the benefits of disability inclusion, with the distribution center experiencing lower turnover rates, higher productivity, and a better safety record than comparable facilities.

The capabilities approach offers a compelling framework for understanding the business case for disability inclusion, highlighting how creating an inclusive workplace enables companies to achieve better financial performance, improved productivity, and a larger customer base. In addition, evidence from the Accenture report, DuPont longitudinal study, and Randy Lewis's experience demonstrate the benefits of disability inclusion. This underscores the fact that it is the right thing to do and a smart business decision that benefits everyone involved.

However, people with disabilities continue to face significant barriers to full participation in the workforce, resulting in lower employment rates and higher unemployment rates than the general public. For example, in 2020, the labor force participation rate for people with disabilities was only 18.7 percent, compared to 61.4 percent for people without disabilities, with people with disabilities experiencing significantly higher unemployment rates at 12.6 percent compared to 6.0 percent for people without disabilities. Nonetheless, people with disabilities possess unique capabilities and strengths that can be valuable to the workforce, including problem-solving, adaptability, resilience, and a unique perspective that can contribute to a more inclusive and diverse workplace.

People with disabilities face significant financial challenges due to their inequitable employment outcomes, including income inequality, lower rates of homeownership, and fewer assets and wealth. To address these challenges, it is essential to accelerate the inclusion of people with disabilities in the workforce and reduce the barriers they face to full participation. Successful large-scale change requires government, corporations, nonprofits, and individual collaboration. The book *Forces for Good* emphasizes the need for these sectors to work together toward a common goal.

The government is critical in providing resources and support to enable people with disabilities to find employment. The

Rehabilitation Services Administration (RSA) and the US vocational rehabilitation system provide vocational training, job placement, and other services to individuals with disabilities. The National Employment Team, a part of the Council of State Administrators of Vocational Rehabilitation (CSAVR), focuses on helping people with disabilities find meaningful employment. The Office of Disability Employment Policy (ODEP) and the Veterans Administration (VA) are other examples of government agencies that offer resources to support individuals with disabilities in finding employment. The Work Opportunity Tax Credit also incentivizes employers to hire people with disabilities.

In conclusion, accelerating the inclusion of people with disabilities in the workforce is essential for improving their financial well-being and reducing inequitable employment outcomes. Collaboration among the government, corporations, nonprofits, and individuals is critical to achieve this. Government agencies such as the RSA, CSAVR, ODEP, VA, and the Work Opportunity Tax Credit can provide resources and support to enable people with disabilities to find employment.

Corporations committed to hiring people with disabilities can leverage resources such as Disability:IN, a nonprofit that provides guidance and tools to support disability inclusion in the workplace. Disability:IN works with corporations to promote best practices, create training programs, and connect employers with talented individuals with disabilities. Nonprofit organizations such as community-based rehabilitation programs can also play a critical role in helping people with disabilities find employment.

Some notable nonprofits that are particularly successful in placing people with disabilities into employment include the National Organization on Disability, the Autism Self Advocacy Network, and the Job Accommodation Network. Grassroots advocacy groups focused on accelerating the employment of people with disabilities are also an important part of the equation. Prominent individual disability advocates include Haben Girma, Chai Feldblum, and Rebecca Cokley. These advocates help raise awareness, promote legislative change, and inspire others to take action.

The alignment and collaboration of government, corporations, nonprofits, and individuals are essential for accelerating the inclusion of people with disabilities in the workforce. With the support of these different sectors, meaningful progress can be made toward a more diverse, equitable, and inclusive workplace for all. Unfortunately, people with disabilities face numerous barriers to achieving inclusion and a sense of belonging in the workplace.

One of the most significant barriers is stigma, leading to misperceptions about their abilities and potential contributions to the workforce. Many people with disabilities are often viewed through a lens of pity or as inspirational figures rather than as capable professionals who can excel in their chosen fields. Myths, prejudices, and discrimination about people with disabilities also contribute to the exclusion of this population from the workforce.

Employers can take several practical steps to increase disability inclusion in the workplace. First, they can review their job descriptions and requirements to ensure they are inclusive and accessible to people with disabilities. Second, they can actively recruit individuals with disabilities through partnerships with disability-focused organizations and job fairs. Third, they can provide reasonable accommodations to enable employees with disabilities to perform their job duties effectively, such as assistive technology, flexible work arrangements, and job coaches. Fourth, they can foster an inclusive work culture by promoting disability awareness and education, providing employee resource groups, and celebrating the contributions of people with disabilities. By taking these steps, employers can create an inclusive and accessible workplace that benefits everyone.

Another crucial aspect of disability inclusion in the workplace is the creation of accessible technology. Many people with disabilities rely on technology to perform their job duties, access information, and communicate with colleagues. Therefore, employers should ensure that their technology and digital platforms are accessible to individuals with disabilities, including those who are blind or have low vision, deaf or hard of hearing, or have physical or cognitive disabilities. This can involve providing screen readers, captioning, and accessible design features. By creating accessible technology, employers can improve the workplace experience for employees with disabilities and enable them to be more productive and successful in their roles.

Disability inclusion in the workplace is not only the right thing to do but also makes good business sense. By creating a culture of inclusion and accessible workplaces, employers can benefit from a more diverse and productive workforce, improved financial performance, and a stronger reputation as a socially responsible company. In addition, by taking practical steps to recruit, retain, and support people with disabilities, and by creating accessible technology and digital platforms, employers can create a more inclusive and accessible workplace that benefits everyone.

Companies can take several practical steps to increase the employment of people with disabilities in their organizations. The following are some actionable recommendations:

1. Include disabilities in your DEI statement: Explicitly state your commitment to creating a diverse and

inclusive workplace that welcomes and accommodates individuals with disabilities. This will convey to your employees, customers, and stakeholders that your organization values disability inclusion.

2. Form a disability-related employee resource group (ERG): Empower your employees with disabilities to connect, collaborate, and share their experiences and perspectives. ERGs can help foster a sense of community and belonging, support, and drive positive change within your organization.

3. Establish a centralized accommodations budget and processes: Invest in accommodations that enable your employees with disabilities to perform their jobs effectively. A centralized accommodations budget and processes will ensure that accommodations are consistently and fairly provided to employees who need them.

4. Require your vendors to provide accessible services and products: Challenge your vendors to create accessible products and services that meet the needs of individuals with disabilities. By requiring accessibility, you're sending a message to your vendors that disability inclusion is a priority.

5. Join forces with other organizations committed to disability inclusion by partnering with Disability:IN or other disability organizations. Reach out to like-minded companies to collaborate, learn from each other, share best practices, and drive change on a larger scale.

6. Use the Disability:IN Disability Equality Index (DEI) to assess your organization's disability inclusion efforts and identify areas for improvement. The DEI is a benchmarking tool that measures disability inclusion policies and practices in the workplace.

7. Invite a qualified professional with disabilities to join your board of directors. By including individuals with

disabilities at the highest levels of your organization, you bring a unique perspective to your decision-making process and demonstrate your commitment to disability inclusion.

8. Partner with community-based nonprofits with a proven track record of placing and supporting individuals with disabilities in the workforce. These organizations can provide valuable guidance, support, and resources to help you to create a more inclusive workplace.

9. Access job seekers with disabilities who are ready, willing, and able to work by partnering with your state's vocational rehabilitation agency and the National Employment Team. These agencies can provide various services and support to help you successfully hire and retain employees with disabilities.

10. Co-create career pathways for people with disabilities by collaborating with stakeholders from various sectors. By working together, you can identify opportunities to address systemic barriers, create more inclusive hiring practices, and build a more diverse and talented workforce.

By taking these steps, you can create a workplace that values and welcomes individuals with disabilities and accelerate the inclusion of people with disabilities in your workforce. Together, we can create a more equitable and inclusive society for all.

There is a strong business case for disability inclusion in the workforce. By intentionally including people with disabilities, companies can expect to see improved financial results. According to the Accenture report on the business case for disability inclusion, disability-inclusive companies outperform their peers financially. Specifically, companies with strong disability policies and practices are 28% more likely to out-perform their peers financially.

Moreover, disability-inclusive businesses have access to a larger customer base, as people with disabilities make up a significant portion of the consumer market. The DuPont longitudinal study further underscores the benefits of disability inclusion, showing that employees with disabilities had lower turnover rates, higher attendance rates, and fewer workplace accidents than their non-disabled peers. Such factors contribute to a more productive workforce, significantly improving a company's bottom line.

ABOUT THE AUTHOR

Dr. Kirk Adams is the founder of Innovative Impact LLC and a professional speaker who earned a PhD in leadership and change. He specializes in creating collaborative solutions that increase the employment of people with disabilities by connecting key decision-makers in government, corporate America, the nonprofit sector, and disability advocates.

INTRODUCTION

BY
DAVID CARTER, FORMER NFL ALL-STAR

Welcome to our book on increasing organizational impact through inclusion and accessibility. I look forward to sharing with you our success stories about implementing these principles and fostering an inclusive work environment.

From my experience as a former NFL All-Star, I know the importance of creating a welcoming and supportive atmosphere to maximize success. My teams accomplished great things when we pursued a common goal as a cohesive unit despite our differences.

In this book, we provide insights on how to use inclusion and accessibility to create positive and lasting change in organizations. We discuss how to create an inclusive culture, honor diverse backgrounds, and maximize the potential of an inclusive and accessible workforce.

We also talk about the importance of an inclusive mindset that encourages and supports people from all walks of life. We provide guidance on the fundamental principle of inclusion, which is about hiring employees based on their merit, not just their diversity. Finally, we illuminate innovation and success through the lens of inclusion and accessibility.

Inclusion and accessibility are critical for any organization that wants to advance and thrive in today's global economy. It's imperative for organizations to develop a culture of inclusion and acceptance that allows people from diverse backgrounds to work together and bring their unique perspectives to any challenge. A company's success depends largely on its ability to build solid teams that are both diverse and inclusive. Companies must create an atmosphere where employees feel respected and valued, and where everyone is encouraged to contribute their unique insights.

This book provides tips on how to honor diverse backgrounds, make the most of an inclusive workforce, and foster an environment of inclusion. We also talk about developing an inclusive mindset.

The basic principle of inclusion, which is essential to the success of any organization, is that everyone should be treated equally regardless of their background or identity. This means that everyone should be respected and valued for their special contribution to the organization.

In addition to this principle, organizations must hire employees based on merit, not just diversity. This means that applicants are judged on their qualifications and experience, not on their race, gender, or other personal characteristics. In this way, companies can ensure that they hire the best qualified individuals and create an inclusive work environment.

Companies also need to foster innovation through inclusion and accessibility. This requires openness to new ideas and perspectives that come from different backgrounds and cultures. Such an approach can lead to the development of new and innovative solutions to problems and help companies remain competitive in the global economy.

This book offers insights into creating a culture of inclusion and respect, harnessing the potential of a diverse workforce, hiring for performance, and innovating through inclusion and accessibility. We also discuss the importance of valuing diverse backgrounds and cultivating an inclusive mindset. By following the advice in this book, companies can create an environment that promotes and supports inclusion, increasing the success of the business.

Creating an inclusive workplace is critical for any company that wants to succeed. It's important to recognize the value of diverse backgrounds and perspectives and create an environment where everyone feels safe, respected, and valued.

I hope this book helps you on your journey to create a culture of inclusion and respect. By embracing diverse perspectives and fostering an inclusive workplace, organizations can thrive in the global economy. Thanks for taking the time to learn more about the importance of inclusion and accessibility.

About the Author

David Carter, also known as the 300-Pound Vegan, is a former NFL player who adopted a vegan lifestyle after watching the documentary *Forks Over Knives*. He has since dedicated himself to raising awareness about "food deserts" and the oppression within the food system, speaking at various universities worldwide. As a film producer, David has been involved in popular Netflix documentaries such as *Game Changers* and *What The Health*.

Leadership and Inclusion: Building the Feeling of Value and Value Add

Jason Miller

L eadership isn't just about having the right skills and knowledge; it's also about creating an inclusive, empowering environment that supports everyone's ability to unlock their unique potential. We all know the power of a strong leader, but most business experts have given much less attention to fostering inclusion as a leader. Promoting and influencing inclusion as a leader has an added value that can help prepare your business for future demands around inclusive leadership and business practices. In this chapter, we'll explore how effective leadership can create an atmosphere of inclusion among team members and the community, allowing for true collaboration and creative growth in any company or entrepreneurial effort.

Inclusion has become a critical factor in the success of businesses today. However, leaders must recognize that developing and promoting an environment of inclusion is only the first step. Adding diversity and equity elements will allow for a holistic approach to inclusive leadership. To prepare your business for the future, you must take additional steps to ensure you are well-equipped with inclusive leadership tools and best practices. A leader's ability to foster an inclusive culture and forward-looking approach will create a foundation for long-term growth and success. In doing so, these leaders show the added value of their proactive efforts toward inclusivity, enabling them to stay ahead of the curve regarding emerging needs surrounding inclusion.

Inclusive leadership is an empowering approach encouraging people from all backgrounds to feel included and supported in their environment. It's a positive way of leading that removes obstacles, breaks down barriers, and offers room for growth to those around you. Inclusive leadership is not a one-size fits all concept but a fully customizable way of creating an atmosphere of cooperation and respect. It isn't a general concept but a broad one that looks different in practice from business to business. Each style of inclusive leadership can only meet the needs of some business communities. Inclusive leadership is about letting everyone have a voice in the decision-making process or creating space for every voice to be vocal and share their perspectives and ideas. For proper inclusion to take place, this should happen regardless of gender, nationality, age, or any other distinguishing quality. Bringing in the unique experiences of people from various backgrounds helps us cultivate a culture built upon inclusion and the well-being of each other and our community.

To meet all emerging expectations around inclusive business practices, inclusive leaders must prioritize including people from diverse backgrounds, perspectives, and life experiences. In doing so, they create workplaces that foster a culture of innovation, collaboration, and growth. All team members will feel respected and empowered to contribute meaningfully in an inclusive environment. Inclusion also brings unique insights that can unlock unprecedented opportunities for companies. For example, businesses embracing inclusion can increase their competitiveness, improve employee satisfaction and morale, and increase employee engagement. When maximizing success in the business world, embracing inclusion should always be a part of the equation.

Valuing diversity and bringing together a wide range of perspectives fosters creative problem-solving, encourages collaboration among teams, and allows the tailoring of solutions to the needs of our staff, customers, and community. While this all sounds important, the real question a leader must ask themselves is, how do we accomplish inclusive practice as a leader? Bringing diverse voices to the business table is only as important as how often we listen to, include, and implement those voices and their experiences. Sometimes the voices and experiences are foreign to us because we don't share the same background, but these moments define our ability to be inclusive. How we respond and practice our openness to new information adds value to our efforts as leaders and shows the value-add inclusion brings to business and entrepreneurship.

Inclusion is important because it allows leaders to build relationships with their staff and include their ideas and perspectives. Including new ideas and perspectives leads to a better understanding and a stronger sense of accountability and collaboration among staff, customers, clients, and the leader. In addition, when organizations practice inclusion, it creates a broader talent pool of people who can bring new skills and experiences to help meet multiple challenges and goals. Inclusion in business leadership is an invaluable asset that leads to improved communication, higher employee engagement, and increased business success across industries.

Inclusion and leadership make diversity so valuable, especially in problem-solving. Bringing together various perspectives in a respectful and welcoming environment creates an atmosphere where creativity can thrive. Creativity is a critical element of the role of a business leader and entrepreneur. Creativity is built on so many of our businesses and business ideas. Imagining the expansiveness of creative resources and realizing this can help our businesses thrive and truly stand out in the business world. The best way to tap into our creative resources is to bring creative voices to the drawing board and watch the business ideas flourish.

Alone, our thoughts and creativity can be limited. These limitations are because we only have experiences and dreams to draw from. When we bring other creative leaders to the table, who have experiences different from ours, we can build business practices, values, and beliefs that supersede anything we had imagined our businesses could be before. We can learn much more from each other than we know if we center the practice of bringing diverse voices together and including their ideas and perspectives. This practice alone will help your business grow and find innovative solutions. Bringing various voices to the table can also help your business center the needs of staff, customers, and the community in a meaningful way that meets the needs of these community members. In the spirit of collaboration, we can come together and share our diverse points of view to create an even brighter future.

Inclusive leadership is vital for any organization, as it creates an environment where individuals from all backgrounds and perspectives can thrive. Inclusivity means recognizing the value of everyone's contributions, no matter their job title or position. Leaders should focus on understanding team members' needs while creating an atmosphere of mutual respect. In an inclusive workplace, a leader must ensure that all team members are heard and feel included in decision-making. At its core, being an inclusive leader involves actively listening to diverse perspectives and experiences while valuing them equally. In other words, leaders must ensure that inclusion is discussed and practiced.

Inclusion and its importance in leadership are often overlooked, but it's a fundamental cornerstone of successful business management. Inclusion requires active listening to ensure each individual is heard and their perspective valued. To be an effective leader, you must seek different experiences and views while maintaining impartiality towards them, recognizing each opinion as having equal value. In this way, you'll not only create an open-minded environment but also have access to a more innovative range of ideas. You cannot just listen; you must also act. An essential part of fostering inclusion is being open to hearing about differences and being available to implement change around business challenges and needs. Working on inclusion is just as crucial and ultimately brings innovation and new solutions to challenges because diverse experiences can tackle challenges and needs in various ways. In short, leaders must strive for true inclusion to achieve the best possible outcome.

Inclusion can be tricky to foster, but it's essential for any successful business. Leaders must be open to listening to the voices of their teams, hearing about different perspectives and experiences, taking actionable steps to implement new ideas, and taking steps towards creating genuine inclusion in business objectives. Inclusive leadership involves more than just talking the talk; it's about walking the walk and actively engaging with people on how their roles translate into the larger vision. Inclusive leadership should also include mentorship and bringing people into the business world who may need more opportunities to do so. These actions matter to an inclusive leader. To establish an environment where everyone can come together and make their best contributions, leaders must prioritize empathy and accessibility when thinking through solutions that better serve all employees. In this way, differences are not seen as something to be feared but as opportunities for creativity in problem-solving that can lead to much more significant successes for everyone involved.

Inclusion isn't just a buzzword. When used correctly, it has incredible benefits for businesses of all sizes. Even the most challenging tasks become easy in an office environment where everyone feels seen and respected. Inclusive workplaces foster creativity by tapping into the ideas of various employees while empowering leadership helps identify problems before they even happen. Promoting inclusion leads to greater business efficiency, higher employee morale and engagement, and improved relationships in your business community. It even supports better reviews of your business and higher customer satisfaction. Embracing the power of inclusion can do wonders for a business.

Inclusion can revolutionize how businesses operate on an interpersonal level. Our efforts to center inclusion as a core element of our business ethos can also change how we interact with the world. When inclusion becomes a core element or practice in our lives can have a lasting impact on us as business owners and human beings. This way, inclusion work and leading with inclusion at heart can be transformative. When leaders strive for inclusiveness, multiple benefits go beyond just innovation. The result is also often increased efficiency for the company, higher employee and customer engagement, and more positive relationships with those in the immediate business community. Inclusion allows ideas to be heard from every corner of an organization, meaning more forms of inspiration and collaboration when planning strategies. When we center inclusion, we model this critical value for other businesses and encourage others to join us in our efforts to make inclusive leadership the standard in business. Modeling and implementing inclusion can lead to more significant successes and open up opportunities for collaboration between companies that may have yet to be explored. Inclusion can be a mighty force in any business endeavor.

Some business owners and entrepreneurs may view inclusive leadership practices as risky or overly ambitious. Inclusion practices can feel intimidating for businesses that have not considered it an asset to their work. However, the goal for an inclusive-minded leader is to view inclusive practice and leadership as the cornerstone of your business modus operandi or operations. To reach the highest echelons of business success, businesses should embrace inclusion as their most coveted value and recognize its importance to our ever-evolving social norms. Our companies rely on those who invest their time, interest, and finances into our business. These are typically the customers of our companies and our greater community of supporters and investors. As business owners, we must understand that our success depends on our ability to connect with our customers and the community our business serves. In a world where diversity and inclusion are making their way to the forefront, we must follow suit for the prospect of a successful business experience. Inclusive leadership is about the practices we believe in and the practices our communities expect and desire from us. We can find balance in both. By setting this critical example as a business, we can encourage other leaders to chart their paths toward building a better and more inclusive society. We're not just sending a message; we're exhibiting what excellence looks like when we give every member of our team and the business community equal opportunity, support, and resources to thrive. Inclusion has always been radical, but now it can be revolutionary.

Inclusion is the key to success in any business, large or small. To create an inclusive environment and maximize productivity, it is essential that leadership at every level actively works to foster acceptance of others. Promoting acceptance and inclusion is easy to understand. However, fostering inclusion can feel more daunting or challenging for business owners and entrepreneurs. It's important to remember that even when the work of inclusive leadership feels challenging, creating a workplace and business environment that supports true inclusion is a worthy effort. Not only is it ethically sound, but it also is essential for standing out as a business leader and setting an industry standard around how your business plans to meet the moment of today's expectations of inclusion and future expectations for social change.

Fostering inclusion as a business leader means ensuring fair and caring practices for your staff and business. These practices might look like promotion opportunities for your team, getting to know employees personally by building meaningful connections and addressing unconscious bias through employee training. Implementing these practices can look like bringing in consultants or walking your employees through self-paced training. As a business leader, you can also consider implementing an accessible complaint system so workers can voice their concerns. It's essential to implement these changes with customers and your business community. Asking for customer feedback can offer insight into your business's community needs and expectations, especially regarding the inclusive nature of what you do. Remember, what we do as leaders will always impact our customer base. Our customers can sense and feel if we are a business that cares about inclusion or a business that does not care at all. Inclusion is essential to and for every aspect of the company and its more significant impact.

In addition to some of the listed suggestions for inclusive leadership practices, business leaders should prioritize work-life balance. Prioritizing work-life balance means you create a work-life balance for yourself and expect it from your staff. Modeling these practices is the best way to standardize them. Depending on the size of your business and your business priorities, you can also consider providing competitive benefits packages for your staff that genuinely allow them to take care of themselves and their families. Hosting social activities and volunteer opportunities for employees and your business community is also an excellent way to foster inclusive practice as a business owner. It helps develop connections while also emphasizing the importance of caring for others. What we see as business and what we understand as our personal lives overlap, and it's okay to lead into this and maximize the interconnectedness of our lives to help support our business efforts. These examples are the essential building blocks for inclusion in the workplace. Through proper implementation of these strategies, businesses can ensure that their organization feels the full power of inclusion and ultimately experience tremendous success.

ABOUT THE AUTHOR

Jason "The Bull" Miller is a seasoned CEO with over twenty years of experience mentoring business owners and excelling in project management, company growth, and strategic implementation. He operates The Strategic Advisor Board, Miller & Company, and multiple other businesses. The author of ten international bestselling books, Jason donates all book sales to "Homes for Heroes."

Fostering an Inclusive and Accessible Workplace Through Mindful Communication

Chris O'Byrne

Effective communication lies at the heart of strong business leadership, and its significance in fostering an inclusive and accessible workplace cannot be overstated. This chapter delves into the critical role of mindful communication in promoting diversity, equity, and inclusion (DEI) within an organization. By developing and implementing communication strategies that consider the diverse needs and preferences of all team members, leaders can create a more inclusive and accessible workplace that maximizes the potential of every employee.

MINDFUL COMMUNICATION: A PILLAR OF DEI

Mindful communication, a concept rooted in mindfulness, emphasizes active listening, empathy, and awareness of one's thoughts, emotions, and biases while engaging in conversation. By consciously adapting their communication styles to meet the needs of their diverse workforce, leaders can create an inclusive environment where all employees feel valued and heard. This section will discuss the importance of active listening, empathy, and self-awareness in mindful communication.

1. **Active listening**

   Active listening is an essential component of mindful communication that involves giving full attention to the speaker and striving to understand their perspective. This practice encourages open-mindedness and demonstrates respect for the speaker's ideas, which can foster an inclusive environment where all employees feel comfortable expressing their thoughts and opinions.

   a. Fostering open-mindedness

      Being open-minded means being receptive to new ideas and perspectives. In a diverse workplace, leaders must exhibit this quality to ensure employees from different backgrounds and experiences feel valued and included. Active listening encourages open-mindedness by requiring the listener to focus on understanding the speaker's point of view without immediately judging or dismissing it.

b. Demonstrating respect

Active listening conveys respect for the speaker and their ideas. Leaders can show their employees that their opinions matter by giving their undivided attention and asking questions to clarify understanding. This respect can increase trust, stronger relationships, and a more inclusive work environment.

2. Empathy

Empathy is the ability to understand and share the feelings of others. By expressing empathy, leaders can bridge gaps in understanding and encourage a supportive, inclusive workplace culture. This can be particularly crucial when addressing issues related to DEI, as empathetic leaders can better recognize their diverse workforce's unique challenges and experiences.

a. Building stronger connections

Empathy helps leaders establish deeper connections with their employees. By understanding and acknowledging their feelings, leaders demonstrate that they genuinely care about their employees' well-being. This emotional connection can increase employee loyalty and a stronger sense of belonging.

b. Navigating conflict resolution

Empathy plays a crucial role in resolving conflicts in a diverse work environment. By understanding the perspectives of all parties involved, leaders can facilitate constructive dialogue and find solutions that address everyone's needs and concerns.

3. Self-awareness

Self-awareness involves recognizing and acknowledging one's thoughts, emotions, and biases. By practicing self-awareness, leaders can identify and address potential barriers to effective communication and create an environment where all employees feel understood and valued.

a. Recognizing unconscious bias

Unconscious biases are automatic, deeply ingrained beliefs or stereotypes about certain groups of people. These biases can negatively impact communication and decision-making, creating an exclusionary work environment. By being self-aware and acknowledging their biases, leaders can take steps to mitigate their influence on their actions and communication.

b. Managing emotions

Emotional self-awareness allows leaders to recognize and manage their emotions effectively. By understanding their feelings, leaders can ensure that their communication remains constructive, respectful, and inclusive, even in challenging situations.

PRACTICAL STRATEGIES FOR MINDFUL COMMUNICATION

The following strategies can help business leaders develop and implement mindful communication practices in their organizations:

1. **Implementing inclusive language**

   Inclusive language aims to respect and acknowledge the diversity of all individuals by avoiding words or phrases that may marginalize or exclude specific groups of people. Leaders should be mindful of the language they use in spoken and written communication and consider adopting inclusive alternatives when appropriate. This can include using gender-neutral terms, avoiding ableist language, and respecting individuals' preferred pronouns.

a. Gender-neutral terms

Using gender-neutral terms, such as "they" or "them" instead of "he" or "she," can help create a more inclusive environment by avoiding assumptions about an individual's gender identity. In addition, using terms like "chairperson" instead of "chairman" or "workforce" instead of "manpower" can promote gender neutrality within the workplace.

b. Avoiding ableist language

Ableist language refers to words or phrases that marginalize or demean individuals with disabilities. By being mindful of ableist language, leaders can ensure that their communication is respectful and inclusive of all employees. For example, instead of using terms like "handicapped" or "disabled," leaders can use "people with disabilities" or "individuals with different abilities."

2. **Offering multiple communication channels**

Multiple communication channels allow employees with different preferences and needs to engage effectively with their colleagues and leaders. In-person meetings, video conferences, phone calls, and written communication should be available to accommodate various communication styles and accessibility needs. This ensures that all employees have an equal opportunity to participate in workplace discussions and decision-making processes.

a. Accommodating communication styles

Employees have different communication styles, and leaders should be mindful of these preferences when selecting communication channels. For example, some employees prefer face-to-face conversations, while others feel more comfortable expressing themselves in writing. By offering multiple communication channels, leaders can accommodate these preferences and ensure all employees feel included and engaged.

b. Accessibility considerations

Providing accessible communication options is essential for creating an inclusive workplace. This includes offering accommodations such as sign language interpreters, real-time captioning, or assistive listening devices for employees with hearing impairments and making written materials available in alternative formats, such as large print or braille, for employees with visual impairments.

1. **Encouraging open dialogue and feedback**

Creating an open dialogue and feedback culture is essential for fostering an inclusive workplace. Leaders should encourage employees to share their thoughts, opinions, and concerns without fear of retribution. This can be achieved by regularly soliciting feedback through anonymous surveys, holding open forums, and providing opportunities for one-on-one discussions.

a. Anonymous surveys

Anonymous surveys can be an effective way to gather honest feedback from employees. By ensuring anonymity, leaders can create a safe space for employees to share their thoughts and concerns about DEI without fear of negative consequences.

b. Open forums

Holding open forums or town hall meetings can give employees a platform to voice their opinions and engage in meaningful discussions about DEI issues. Leaders can foster a culture of open dialogue and inclusion by actively participating in these events and demonstrating a commitment to listening and learning.

2. Training and development

Offering training and development programs focused on mindful communication, and DEI can help employees and leaders improve their communication skills and enhance their understanding of diverse perspectives. These programs should cover unconscious bias, active listening, empathy, and inclusive language and be accessible to all employees.

a. Unconscious bias training

Unconscious bias training helps participants recognize and address their implicit biases, enabling them to communicate more inclusively and effectively with their colleagues. As a result, organizations can create a more inclusive and equitable work environment by providing this training.

b. Active listening and empathy workshops

Workshops focused on active listening and empathy can provide employees with the tools and strategies to communicate more effectively and compassionately with their colleagues. These workshops can help foster a supportive and inclusive workplace culture by teaching participants to understand better and appreciate diverse perspectives.

Mindful communication is an influential tool leaders can use to foster an inclusive and accessible workplace. By actively listening, expressing empathy, and being self-aware, leaders can create an environment where all employees feel valued and heard. Implementing practical strategies such as using inclusive language, offering multiple communication channels, and encouraging open dialogue and feedback can further support this goal.

By prioritizing mindful communication, business leaders not only promote a more inclusive and accessible workplace but also lay the foundation for a thriving organizational culture. Embracing DEI through conscious communication can lead to increased employee satisfaction, improved collaboration, and higher levels of innovation, ultimately resulting in a more prosperous and resilient organization.

In summary, the importance of mindful communication in business leadership cannot be overstated. By cultivating a culture of open dialogue, empathy, and active listening, leaders can ensure that their organizations are inclusive and accessible for all employees, regardless of their background or unique needs. In addition, by investing in developing mindful communication skills and strategies, business leaders can position their organizations for long-term success in an increasingly diverse and interconnected world.

About the Author

Chris O'Byrne is the CEO of JETLAUNCH Publishing and co-owner of the Strategic Advisor Board and Rogue Publishing Partners. He has published over 12,000 books and hundreds have become international bestsellers. He is also the author of 10 international bestsellers.

Building a
Culture of Equity

Patricia Baronowski-Schneider

To me, inclusion means feeling included, and accessibility means being accessible and having access to what is needed.

In contrast to accessibility, inclusiveness offers a range of tools and features that the end user can select to meet their needs in the setting or context. This is where inclusiveness differs from accessibility.

Inclusion aims to embrace everyone, regardless of color, gender, disability, or other needs. It seeks to eliminate prejudice and intolerance while providing fair access to all possibilities (removing barriers).

All facets of public life are affected. When something is accessible, people can complete their tasks with the same time and effort as those who do not have a disability.

Systems must be designed to maximize access as part of accessibility.

Giving everyone the same access and opportunity is a crucial component of inclusivity. In education, this entails removing and surmounting obstacles that could appear in digital materials and activities for teaching and learning.

Accessibility is advantageous for users with disabilities, but it is also helpful for your company.

Accessibility may boost your brand, expand your audience, lower your risk of legal issues, and increase your SEO and usability.

One of the most crucial factors in retention is inclusion in the workplace.

Employees eventually leave an organization if they don't believe their opinions, presence, or contributions are respected or taken seriously.

Diversity, involvement, and belonging are valued in a workplace that is positive and inclusive.

The idea of inclusion in the workplace will always remain prevalent.

Employers must allow employees to be authentic versions of themselves.

The culture of the workplace can be improved by creating an inclusive environment. It conveys a crucial statement about the principles of your business. Employees, including those with and without disabilities, care more and more about the culture of their company and think the company must support their success.

Research shows many of the advantages of a diverse and inclusive workplace. For example:

- More rapid revenue growth
- Increased capacity to attract a diversified talent pool
- Increased capacity to innovate
- Higher staff retention by 5.4 times

One of the most crucial factors in retention is inclusion in the workplace.

Employees will eventually leave an organization if they don't believe their opinions, presence, or contributions are respected or taken seriously.

According to established studies on corporate culture, when workers believe they and their coworkers will be treated equitably regardless of color, gender, sexual orientation, or age…

- They are 9.8 times more likely to anticipate starting work
- There is a 6.3-fold increase in pride in one's work
- They are 5.4 times more likely to wish to remain with their firm for a long time

Creating an inclusive workplace culture will help you gain a varied group of talent, and it will help you keep the diverse talent you already have.

By encouraging a culture of acceptance, tolerance, and accessibility, leadership can have a significant impact on a company. This will enhance working conditions at the company, foster diversity, and make it safer and more welcoming for staff members with impairments. I am also a firm believer in leading by example. If a leader shows inclusion and accessibility, it can trickle down the chain to entice everyone to do the same.

Success depends on inclusive leaders. They help people realize their full potential, strengthen the power of working together in teams, and improve your company's capacity for innovation and expansion.

Here are twenty examples of non-inclusive workplace conduct. Adhering to becoming inclusive can help end these issues.

1. Assuming responsibility for problems instead of taking responsibility for your communication and behavior patterns.
2. Ineffective nonverbal exchanges—avoiding eye contact or acting inattentive and being absent when the contact request is made. This and a closed-door hierarchical policy are closely related.
3. Inappropriate voice tone—a tone of speech that is aggressive, patronizing, condescending, or scornful.
4. Careless listening, talking over, cutting off, or criticizing in public. The "cc all" option is frequently used to publicly disgrace or humiliate someone. While speaking to someone, you are multitasking and not paying attention. Even when you're going through the hallways, have your phone in your pocket, so you can be there for anyone you run into. Nowadays, many organizations forbid using phones during meetings because studies show they reduce productivity.

5. Making assumptions without verifying the information. To better understand the presented problem, pose Socratic questions. Making charges is a different action that frequently occurs after this. For example, "You are perpetually late. You lack motivation for this task and are lazy. Try, "You appear to have trouble keeping track of time. What's happening to you?

6. Playing favorites—not treating individuals equally regardless of color, religion, gender, size, age, personality, or preference. For an inclusive workplace, consistency is crucial.

7. Taking credit for someone else's work and passing it off as your own (known as hijacking someone else's concept). However, owning the concept and delegating the hard labor to the creator is much worse.

8. Any form of bullying or harassment. Bullying, taunting, or harassment motivated by differences in race, religion, gender, body type, age, or nationality. It can also be motivated by personal preferences. The list goes on and on.

9. Abusive language such as yelling, swearing, and insulting people, not using polite language such as please or thank you. The little things are always the ones that count.

10. Remarks or jokes that are not edited. Making jokes or comments about diversity, whether in terms of color, religion, gender, size, gender, age, or nationality. Speaking in a language that others might not understand in a multi-cultural situation.

11. Command-and-control management. Micromanagement is when someone isn't given the freedom to manage their workload or the trust to achieve deadlines. This includes setting arbitrary deadlines as opposed to working together to find a solution.

12. Direct conversation. Gossiping or spreading rumors is the practice of discussing problems behind closed doors or at the water cooler rather than addressing them head-on through a constructive conversation, slandering someone by dropping hints and innuendo.

13. Ignoring or excluding. This includes excluding someone from email chains or meetings and withholding information that would help them succeed. Lack of transparency may be used as a ruse to gain control and manipulate. This is a type of mental exploitation. This also includes withholding personal facts that might enhance your humanity.

14. Offering more criticism than appreciation. Burnout affects both men and women equally, and it frequently results from not being acknowledged.

15. Careless scheduling—arranging events outside of regular business hours that may affect a particular demographic, such as breakfast meetings that will affect parents or failing to consider time zones or regional holidays.

16. Unsuitable themes—organizing awards ceremonies with subjects that will have an adverse effect on a particular group. For instance, rock climbing could have an adverse effect on older employees or those who are less physically fit or serving refreshments with no vegetarian or non-alcoholic options.

17. Acting as a spectator—failing to act as an upstander and conduct an intervention when a certain incident occurs, letting tense situations worsen.

18. Letting ego triumph—concentrating on the corner office and the huge car for self-promotion as symbols of personal authority.

19. Fostering divisiveness rather than unity—putting coworkers up against one another to provide

challenging tasks or outcomes, using ambiguity to one's advantage, and creating circumstances in which someone is made to perform poorly or perhaps fail.

20. Showing disrespect for others' time—talking over others, arriving late for meetings, not accepting responsibility, and blaming the hierarchy, system, or other people.

Equal access and opportunity are part of an inclusive culture for all workers. People with disabilities and other underrepresented groups should be included in an organization's mission statement, rules, and processes. A dedication to diversity and inclusion includes ongoing training for all staff members on disability awareness and inclusivity, as well as return-to-work policies and emergency evacuation protocols that consider the needs of people with disabilities. For instance, employers must have a plan to remove employees in wheelchairs from the upper floors of buildings without the use of elevators.

Offering accessible facilities, services, and products in the workplace is important. All people are encouraged to feel comfortable reporting to work and carrying out their jobs thanks to accommodations.

Employers are now required to ensure that they do not discriminate against job hopefuls or employees because of a person's handicap since the Americans with Disabilities Act (ADA) was passed in 1990.

According to the World Health Organization, 15 percent of people worldwide are disabled. This percentage shows customers who were previously ignored by firms. Accessibility services have recently opened the door for a more inclusive approach to customer and corporate services.

For good reasons, accessibility services are quickly becoming a requirement for businesses to succeed. To begin with, these services encourage diversity and, therefore, broaden reach. Plus, they help prevent lawsuits from occurring. You can end up being lost in the crowd if you decide to stay on the sidelines, given the surge in the adoption of these services by enterprises.

By providing accessible services, you give your company several chances to expand. These services can boost sales, increase brand recognition, and foster client loyalty. You'll be differentiating your company in several ways from its rivals.

It is a win-win for a company to promote inclusion. It also helps keep employees as they feel valued and seen. And by broadening the horizons of the firm, you will bring in an array of talent, which can surely help a business be more competitive.

Here are some thoughts to encourage inclusion, equity, and diversity in the workplace:

- Be mindful of implicit bias
- Promote the value of preventing bias
- Encourage pay equity
- Create a tactical training program
- Recognize all cultural holidays
- Make joining employee resource groups convenient for your staff
- Combine your teams

Regarding embracing accessibility, organizations should ensure that applications are available to all people with disabilities in accessible formats. If at a job fair, they should supply the fair accommodations that eligible candidates would require to compete for the position. You could even hold an employment fair with a disability-specific focus. Companies should also begin teaching everyone at the company—especially managers—how to work with people with impairments.

Although there isn't a single foolproof plan, it's crucial that you and your leaders move toward success. The following are eight methods for accepting diversity at work:

1. Begin the discussion

   Sometimes, it's challenging to choose the best place to begin. The first step in starting a conversation on DEI (Diversity, Equity, and Inclusion) is for leaders to open the door, set the tone, and convey the message. Think about your experience and what you could learn from utilizing greater diversity in your teams.

   What was the turning point when you understood you could embrace diversity? Have you seen or experienced discriminatory behavior? How did it affect things? Use your progressive motion and your experiences.

2. Increase transparency and accountability

   Teams won't feel that enough is being done to make improvements if you don't make it clear what you are doing to raise DEI. An ongoing, open dialogue ensures that efforts are focused on the most crucial areas.

   Think about who is most important in promoting inclusion, equity, and diversity in your organization. (Hint: It's your leaders.) How clearly do you hold your leaders accountable?

3. Improve your leadership abilities

   Do your leaders have the skills? It is not enough to be aware of unconscious prejudice or the commercial case for DEI. Although awareness is a crucial first step, it doesn't always translate into action. To bridge the gap between theory and practice, leaders need a comprehensive strategy for learning the frameworks, tools, and skills they require.

Teaching your leaders how to foster a welcoming environment is one key to achieving that. You can employ innovative and integrated learning techniques to get leaders to think and feel about diversity, equity, inclusion, and accessibility. These strategies include guided sessions, micro-learning, and virtual reality, as examples.

However, too many businesses see inclusion as a distinct skill or extra task, separating it from everything else. Inclusion is not something to use in some circumstances but not others, even though it needs a focus.

It can be included in the daily behaviors that leaders and team members take. Great leadership is inclusive leadership.

4. Note the range of viewpoints expressed during deliberations

Though anybody can suffer the consequences of unconscious bias, certain groups are particularly affected, including women, people of color, those with disabilities, those who speak with accents distinct from the majority, introverts, and those who identify as LGBTQ+.

Decisions about hiring, performance management, delegation, and succession are all affected by bias in very serious ways. To accept diversity, one must first consider who is seated at the table before setting up a varied one.

Leaders must foster an environment where different points of view are represented, aggressively seek those who hold different opinions, distribute authority fairly, and identify chances for everyone's professional growth.

5. Pay attention to how each individual is handled

Virtual and hybrid working environments emphasize our DEI efforts' escalating problems. Amid the epidemic, several minorities have shown that virtual labor has made their homes a safer place with a decrease in discrimination and microaggressions (indirect, subtle, or unintended).

Introverted individuals experience yet another discrepancy. They confess to feeling lost in their screens when questioned, which can make them feel unsupported and jeopardize neurodiversity.

Although flexible employment has many advantages, it also risks increasing and even causing new diversity gaps. Respecting diversity entails being aware of how everyone is handled.

Leaders need to be deliberate. And to do this, one must deliberately interact with each person, affirming their worth through small gestures (both in what they say and in their nonverbal communication).

Above all else, think about what you can do to foster a psychologically secure work atmosphere where everyone feels free to express themselves, be heard, and be themselves.

6. Speak out as an ally

Being an ally is like sparking change. Have you ever seen someone acting in a disrespectful or exclusive way? Have you ever thought there might be a way to enhance DEI? Do you step in to correct injustices you see?

Advocating for others and helping create fair working circumstances are both achieved through embracing diversity. Being an ally is even more important when assisting historically marginalized communities dealing with difficulties.

For instance, women who struggle to climb the leadership ladder encounter inequality. Having supporters who can support them in developing networks, becoming more visible, amplifying their voices, and making sure credit is given properly is extremely beneficial for women.

Acting with courage and sensitivity is required in this situation. To address their exclusionary actions or statements and offer candid, sympathetic feedback, allies may need to call in individuals.

A debate can be redirected to be more inclusive when allies discover strategies to keep participants accountable for creating inclusiveness and respect.

7. Take stock and resolve to change

   Examining oneself is a necessary step in fostering a culture of diversity, equity, and inclusion. Consider your leadership potential and abilities as they relate to these behaviors and practices, while also learning about leadership methods and practices.

   Learning alone is insufficient. Action is what inclusion is all about. Make a commitment based on these self-insights and solicit feedback.

8. Base your platform on psychological safety, feedback, and empathy

   Everyone must take part in embracing diversity; this endeavor involves individuals, teams, and organizations. If socializing calling-in behavior is necessary, keep in mind that it may feel awkward at first. Teams may also find it challenging if feedback is not yet effective or ingrained in the culture.

   When speaking up, teams may be afraid of being disciplined or worried about how others will react. Everyone engaged should be thoughtful of others by upholding their coworkers' self-esteem and exhibiting empathy. After all, not all microaggressions are deliberate. The key is empathy.

Your teams are undoubtedly giving it their all as they work toward equality as part of this improvement journey. However, you may disseminate the idea that people can always do better by acting as a leader. Leaders need to cultivate their own feedback receptivity and set an example of the behaviors they wish to see in their teams. The creation of psychological safety is becoming a top priority in teams because of embracing diversity in the workplace.

Nowadays, the world is changing, and I am happy that this topic requires a change. Everyone needs to be accepted and included—no matter what. I am glad to see this is the direction of change.

From a marketing standpoint, I always stress to clients: How are you different? What makes you better than everyone else? It's not about you; it's about your audience/clients/investors/the world, so how is what you are doing benefitting them?

This is valuable food for thought. First, not everyone with a disability is bad for your business. Did you know that Hawking was one of the most well-known physicists in the world, yet he was diagnosed with ALS when he was 21? Helen Adams Keller was an American author, disability rights advocate, political activist, and lecturer. Born in West Tuscumbia, Alabama, she lost her sight and her hearing after a bout of illness at 19 months old. Stevland Hardaway Morris, known professionally as Stevie Wonder, is an American singer-songwriter who is credited as a pioneer and influencer by musicians across a range of genres that include rhythm and blues, pop, soul, gospel, funk, and jazz.

Having a disability isn't negative. Everyone should be treated with equality and inclusion and have access to all the opportunities everyone else has. If you hire people, regardless of their disability, and they bring in immense talent, isn't that best for your business? If you are inviting this brilliant talent and not looking at disabilities as something negative, won't this help set a higher standard for how your business is perceived? If people see your business as a grander version of everyone else, won't that bring in customers, employees, investors, etc., over your competitors?

Try to stand out from the crowd. Be better than everyone else. And don't look at anyone as different or incapable. Look at everyone as unique, and you'll be surprised at what doors will open for you.

About the Author

Patricia Baronowski-Schneider in an IR/PR/marketing expert who works in driving brand awareness for her clients through integrated marketing. She is a two-time bestselling author with over thirty years of experience working with all types of niches around the world.

TRANSFORMING THE WORKPLACE THROUGH INCLUSION AND ACCESSIBILITY

IRA BOWMAN

People tend to overcomplicate things. Inclusion and accessibility are pretty simple because if your organization is inclusive, it's not restrictive. It's open. Everybody has a fair chance to be part of the company or organization. Accessibility means you provide things like ADA, where you're trying to help accommodate everyone. For example, there's an audio version for the blind, there's a larger printout for the deaf who can't hear. Accommodating disabilities can be as simple as a ramp to get into a building or something similar.

Providing translators is a good option for people who may not speak the language as a native. Materials are available in a variety of languages, so accessibility and inclusion do not exclude anyone by any criteria. Of course, in many situations there's a certain level of prerequisite skills or maybe a college degree of some sort, or maybe you have to have a certificate of completion for this or that, to meet the minimum standard of eligibility. These qualification requirements can reduce the number of people who can take part. Some who are excluded may be capable, but they don't have the qualifications. The goal should be to set the minimum standards in just the way it sounds, the bare minimum needed and then allow as many as possible the opportunity to try. So, to me, inclusion is being as open as possible, and you're only limiting candidates to apply by what is absolutely necessary to get the job done.

It is really important in the workplace to have inclusion and accessibility, at least in the sense of fairness. I think that is probably the most important reason, the sense of fairness, but also beyond fairness as a foundation, you can get ideas that aren't expected. You can come up with solutions that are completely atypical. They're not commonplace; they're not industry standard if you give more people the opportunity to take part. So if you're open to suggestions and you include them, you increase the reach and the potential solutions that are presented. And I think that's very important for the long-term health and success of any company or organization.

Inclusion also helps to foster a real community, a connected-ness, an affinity for the organization, the event, or the group, because nobody feels excluded because of their identity, right be it because of their race, religion, sexual preference, or disabil-ity. Those who feel they have been disadvantaged aren't likely to want to stay and, frankly, won't have positive thoughts or feelings about that organization, company, or group because they feel disadvantaged. So inclusion is important to promote fairness and ideas, to move things forward. Inclusion can manifest in the form of reducing overhead or costs. It can increase revenue, increase participation in the audience, or expand the audience because someone had an idea, a suggestion, or an experience that contributed to the greater good because they were a part of the conversation or the activity or at least participated. That's a good thing.

Inclusion and accessibility are important for a leader for several reasons. First, it sets a good precedent or example for others to follow. Narrow-minded people who only hang out with people who are like them, who think like them, who talk like them, who dress like them, and all those things, have a limited knowledge base and probably have little new to offer because it's always the same thing. But also, when people see you as a leader, they think, well, they only have their inner circle. They're very limited with who can even have access to that inner circle. I don't think that's the right path for you to take as a leader, especially in today's world, where people have a victim mentality and are looking for ways to be offended. I think if you don't have good inclusion and you're not accessible as a leader, the liability of your organization is higher.

There are positives to being inclusive and open, and there are negative legal consequences that may come. But even if it's not a legal cost, there's an opportunity cost because there's a risk whether or not it happens. If you're open and you have a diverse team and you're willing to invite people who think and act differently than you, you allow them to make their case even if you don't take their advice. Just the fact that they're heard lets them know they belong, their equal access to you speaks volumes.

There is a healthy mentality when the dissenting or minority voice is still a part of the process. When they're heard, they're allowed to express their wishes, objections, and views. They help to shape the conversation. If you allow minority voices and opinions to be heard, those people will be more likely to follow you. You're less likely to get involved in litigation, and I think you're also less likely to get boycotted because you're still giving people the opportunity to take part in the discussion. It's important for people not to feel left out, especially considering the culture we live in today and the mindset that's prevalent. Many people are looking for a reason to be offended. Many are looking for validation of their victim mentality. Leaders need to at least be aware of this. You can counteract that by being more inclusive and making accessibility open and not restricted. Truly listening to other opinions can go a long way to making the world a better place.

Promoting inclusion and accessibility in the workplace can be done in several ways, and it starts with hiring practices. People should not be excluded based only on their background; equal opportunity in hiring is a large part of creating true workforce diversity. Inclusion can start there, but it can also blossom with promotions. The end-all-be-all of workforce diversity is not necessarily just about hiring practices; it also involves promotion practices. In the company's marketing, both internal and external, there are different voices and committees with a variety of people, not necessarily just managers or just technicians, but inclusion.

The CEO, the president, the owner, or whoever is steering the ship should be articulating the vision and then getting buy-in from internal departments, allowing them to hear the vision and then bringing forward suggestions or potential concerns in an open forum and also in social media, advertising, and marketing. Again, communicate internally and externally. Have a variety of voices, not just one person who always sounds the same. Not only a spokesperson or a PR person who does all the talking but interviewing the diversity of their workforce. Not just an HR interview where they feel like they're getting people in trouble, but serious, performance-based interviews. Also, random interviews where people discuss what they think is wrong and what they could do better.

What do you do with all of this information? Your organization should have some kind of committee that monitors these conversations and takes action when needed, whether it's correcting mistakes or implementing new ideas that your team comes up with. That encourages people to speak up and not just suffer in silence, which nobody wants. To encourage inclusion, people need to feel comfortable and safe, and they need to feel their job isn't in jeopardy. If they say something that goes against the prevailing opinion in the organization, they don't have to face backlash or retaliation, and this promotes inclusion. And with social media, with the internal and external marketing component, showing different people in different departments, no matter what their race, religion, or worldview. It's kind of a rainbow campaign, showing employees and workers who are brand new and those who have been there forever, both management and workers. That helps you promote accessibility and inclusion because people feel they're part of a real organization and not just voiceless drones.

Promoting inclusion and accessibility improves a company's competitiveness. With an inclusive environment, you have more diversity, and the knowledge base is larger. You are more competitive because you get solutions faster and get to market faster. There's less opportunity for failure because not only are the ideas behind the solutions you bring to market broader but there's more experience to avoid potential pitfalls.

In an inclusive environment, where accessibility is open as much as possible, and people with disabilities can take part, there's also an affinity for the company or the organization. People are more willing to put up with things they don't like and minor dissatisfaction because they love where they work. You don't have to keep putting income or revenue into training new people, which means fewer starts and stops. If people love their job and stay longer, they're more likely to talk positively about their work in the community, and so it creates a ripple effect.

With a company where there's constant turnover, people are less likely to want to work there, even if they pay more. That company gets a reputation for being toxic, which can ultimately be the downfall of the company. But an inclusive, approachable company, that kind of environment provides stability and allows you to build solid relationships with competitors. When you're competing with people who have been around longer and are better because they have more experience, the quality goes up, whether it's a service or a product. Customer service is better, and their reputation increases. The brand's reputation depends on the people who provide it. If employees are in an environment where they feel valued, they'll do a better job in all areas.

All of that contributes to companies being more competitive, especially when they're not constantly wasting money on hiring new people because they have an established employee base. They also have more money to invest, whether it's in research and development or vacation time or bonuses. The company runs better and will provide better service or a better product than a company that isn't well run and has high turnover, has problems with leadership, isn't inclusive, and doesn't want to hear contrary opinions or ideas. That kind of environment doesn't foster a competitive workforce, and performance suffers, and so do the products and services you bring to market. It's smart to promote inclusion and accessibility.

For a company that hasn't been good at making inclusion and accessibility a reality in the past, this may be hard. Fixing a system that has been toxic or has failed will take a lot of work. You'll probably need to bring in an outside leader, such as a consultant, or hire new management. But inclusion and accessibility need to be more than just lip service. Information needs to be shared throughout the organization. There should be some clear promises that say, "Hey, this is who we are, and this is what we're about."

Accessibility can mean access to advancement, access to communication without blame or retribution, and access to whatever is needed to do a great job. Has your company done a good job of accommodating disabilities or struggles, or meeting people's needs for flexible hours or working from home?

Your policies should be clearly stated in your employee handbook or as part of the HR documents. It needs to be in writing, and it needs to be available to everyone in the company or organization. Everybody who works in the company, from a new employee to the CEO and everybody in between, should have access to that promise that you are committed to this. It could be an announcement video or a conversation that's had in a company-wide meeting. It could be disseminated by department heads. It could be a letter or an email that's sent out, but the foundation for that is the HR documentation. If you're starting a company from scratch, you can talk about it while interviewing potential employees or when you're onboarding new employees. It starts with HR, but then the management team has to make sure that it's embraced.

If you haven't considered inclusion and accessibility in your organization, I challenge you to bring in an outsider to make suggestions or at least consider doing surveys. Do a blind survey where employees don't have to worry about backlash and ask them how the company is doing with inclusion and accessibility. Ask what would make it better. And then, set aside your ego and make real change based on that feedback from the people who make up your organization.

It's worth the struggle, and it's worth the cost, the cost of infrastructure, or whatever you need to do to change your hiring practices and your leadership style and change the way you lead your people. Listen to your people. It's worth it because employees are the strength of the company, the backbone of the company, and they can bring you down as fast as they can build you up. Invest in them and make them feel wanted, make them feel heard, and give them everything they need to contribute fully. You'll see it is worth the time and money you invest in making it better. The effort will help your business thrive and become more successful, better positioned to sustain success into the future.

ABOUT THE AUTHOR

Professionally, Ira is a marketing and sales expert, photographer, graphics designer, website builder, philanthropy owner, search engine optimization content writer, and TEDx speaker. Ira has built a large social media following with six-figure following counts on both LinkedIn and Instagram.

Overcoming Barriers in the Workplace for People with Disabilities

Dr. Julie Ducharme

It has been about fifteen years since I last worked with people with disabilities. When I took that job, I didn't realize what I was walking into, but it was one of my most enlightening experiences. The organization I applied to work with as a consultant for building an adaptive computer lab was unique.

I had never heard of a place like this before. They helped individuals with developmental disabilities discover, explore, and nurture their potential, giving them a chance to live their lives to the fullest. This group supported people who were autistic, had Down syndrome, or were physically or mentally disabled. They offered services ranging from job training and workforce integration to learning, gardening, swimming classes, art programs, and much more.

When I started working with them, I quickly realized I did not understand people with physical or mental disabilities or how talented, smart, and truly amazing they were. Unfortunately, society has often minimized these individuals as unintelligent, limited, and unable to interact with others successfully. To my surprise, not only was I wrong, but so was society.

I observed first hand how my bias and that of society in general caused me not to be inclusive of people with disabilities. Despite all our technological advances, inclusion, and equality, we still carry stereotypes and misinformation about how these individuals can be integrated into the workplace. Sadly, even with as much education as we can offer, I believe there will always be a struggle to include those who are different and whom we don't understand.

When I began designing the computer lab and working with these students daily, I quickly learned they were incredibly smart but faced limitations due to outdated technology. For example, they lacked adaptive technology, such as specific types of mice and keyboards, that would allow them to better navigate computers because of physical limitations in their hands. In addition, some students had visual or hearing impairments and required magnifying programs or special headsets.

Others suffered from chronic seizures, necessitating the use of flat screen monitors, as the old monitors triggered seizures—a surprising fact, but one that is supported by case studies. Fifteen years ago, adaptive technology was difficult to find because it wasn't recognized as a need, so it wasn't being produced.

As I sat in a room filled with intelligent, disabled, and frustrated individuals, I realized they were just like you and me. They loved to dance, had favorite music groups, and favorite books. They discussed politics and the lack of laws supporting them and providing opportunities. My world was rocked, and I was embarrassed I had allowed this negative view of special needs individuals to persist in my mind, leading me to be non-inclusive due to my ignorance.

I share this because we, as leaders, may not recognize our lack of inclusivity when we're not educating ourselves and operating based on a false narrative. I thought I was a good leader by not hiring someone with a disability, believing it would be unfair and they wouldn't be able to keep up. I was wrong, but building an adaptive computer lab for these uniquely challenged individuals allowed me to compensate for my ignorance.

In this chapter, I address the lack of inclusion and accessibility for disabled individuals, whether physical or mental. Many people fall into this category, either from birth or due to events in their lives, such as veterans of our armed services who are injured and become disabled while serving. I shared earlier how I was also guilty of being non-inclusive fifteen years ago, but I educated myself and am now an advocate for the disabled.

Even now, our biases and views toward people with disabilities persist. Although these attitudes have been somewhat minimized with the help of technology, we still have a lot of work to do. First, let's explore what inclusion means. Inclusion refers to creating a welcoming and supportive environment for all individuals, regardless of their background, identity, or abilities. It involves actively working to remove barriers and promoting diversity and equity.

Accessibility, however, focuses on ensuring that products, services, and environments are designed to allow people of all abilities to use and enjoy them. This means considering the needs of individuals with disabilities, including physical, sensory, and cognitive disabilities, and providing accommodations and support to ensure they can fully participate in society.

In summary, both inclusion and accessibility are about recognizing and valuing the differences that exist between individuals. The goal is to work toward creating a society that is genuinely inclusive and accessible to everyone, including people with disabilities.

Inclusion and accessibility are essential in the workplace for several reasons. First, they improve diversity and representation. Inclusion means creating an environment that values diversity and promotes equity. By doing so, companies can attract a broader range of talent, including individuals from underrepresented groups.

Often, our disabled population is incredibly smart and talented, but accessibility is the issue. For example, public bus transportation might also be difficult if driving is not an available option. The office may not be set up for the handicapped, such as the office desk setup and movability around the room. Even if there is a handicapped stall in the bathroom, perhaps the bathroom is a long walk to get to.

Some of these issues may be unavoidable because they are inherent to the layout of the office or location, and the owners can't do much about it. However, I believe there is always a way to adapt the office to include our brilliant yet disabled individuals. This leads to a more diverse workforce that brings a variety of perspectives and experiences to the table, which can result in better problem-solving and innovation.

Increased productivity and innovation are other benefits of fostering inclusion and accessibility in the workplace. Employees who feel included and valued are more likely to be engaged and productive. They are also more likely to feel comfortable sharing their ideas and opinions, which can lead to innovations and solutions.

When working with my disabled students, I discovered how inclusive they were of me. They accepted me immediately, even though I initially felt uncomfortable because I wasn't sure how to interact with them. I soon learned that they loved to laugh and would frequently tease me, albeit innocently. They even made light of their disabilities.

I discovered that I didn't need to tiptoe around them, as they were not fragile. Several were married and lived on their own or with the help of someone if their physical disabilities were difficult to manage. I even met a couple who was disabled, had two non-disabled children, and the husband worked—a beautiful family. But, like everyone else, I realized they wanted to feel valued and included. They even told me they didn't want special treatment or to be treated like a child; they just needed accessibility to do their work.

Better retention rates are another advantage of promoting inclusion and accessibility in the workplace. Employees are likely to stay with a company that values their contributions and creates an inclusive and accessible environment. This can help reduce turnover and save on recruitment and training costs.

Legal compliance is also important. In many countries, including the United States, employers have legal requirements to provide equal opportunities and accommodations for individuals with disabilities. Failure to comply with these laws can lead to legal consequences and negative publicity. Although the Americans with Disabilities Act was enacted in 1990 by George Bush, prompting the retrofitting of offices, bathrooms, and sidewalks to support disabled individuals and leading to the development of some revolutionary technology, there is still much work to be done.

Inclusion and accessibility are crucial for cultivating a positive workplace culture that values diversity, promotes equity, and fosters innovation and productivity.

As a leader, inclusion and accessibility are important for several reasons:

First, they set the tone for the organization. Leaders are responsible for establishing the tone for the organization, and creating a culture of inclusion and accessibility starts at the top. When leaders model inclusive behavior, they send a message to their employees that these values are important and valued within the organization.

When I started working with veterans as a leader, I saw the same struggle as with my disabled students. These brilliantly trained men and women were adaptable and could handle high-stress situations but often had physical disabilities or other issues resulting from war. As a result, they needed accommodations, such as a quiet place to work, easy access, or flexibility in getting to the office if they relied on public transportation.

I implemented policies like flexible work hours and remote work options to address these challenges. This created a positive culture, a more adaptable work environment, and happier employees. They felt less threatened by the lack of inclusion and empowered by my flexibility and willingness to recognize their skills, understanding that their disabilities should not detract from their ability to work.

Encouraging innovation and creativity is another reason leaders should prioritize inclusion and accessibility. Diversity of thought and experience is crucial for fostering innovation and creativity. Leaders who create an inclusive and accessible workplace can help cultivate an environment where diverse perspectives are encouraged, leading to new ideas and solutions.

One of the things I appreciate about working with disabled veterans and employees with physical or mental disabilities is their unique perspectives. They bring a distinct, positive viewpoint that has helped improve my business. They see things through a different lens, and by doing so, they increase my client base as they teach me how to be more inclusive and innovative, especially in technology. A company's success lies in its ability to innovate better and faster than its competitors, which cannot be achieved with groupthink.

Demonstrating social responsibility is another aspect of prioritizing inclusion and accessibility. These values are important in society, and leaders who emphasize them show their commitment to social responsibility. This can help improve the organization's reputation and attract socially conscious employees, customers, and investors.

Mitigating legal risks is another important reason leaders prioritize inclusion and accessibility. As mentioned earlier, employers have legal requirements to provide equal opportunities and accommodations for individuals with disabilities. Leaders focusing on inclusion and accessibility can help ensure the organization complies with these laws, reducing the risk of legal consequences.

Inclusion and accessibility can help solve a variety of problems in the workplace, including:

Discrimination and bias: An inclusive workplace culture values diversity and promotes equity, reducing the likelihood of discrimination and bias in the workplace. Discrimination will exist in some form, no matter where you go or how hard you work, as it is just human nature.

Lack of diversity: Inclusion can help attract and retain a more diverse workforce, leading to various perspectives and experiences that can help solve problems in new and innovative ways.

Low employee engagement: When employees feel excluded or undervalued, their motivation and engagement in their work can suffer. Prioritizing inclusion and accessibility helps to increase employee engagement and job satisfaction.

Poor communication: When employees come from different backgrounds and experiences, communication can be challenging. An inclusive workplace culture can promote open communication and respect for different perspectives, helping to improve communication and collaboration.

Inefficient processes: Accessibility can help ensure that all employees can participate in the workplace, regardless of their physical, sensory, or cognitive abilities. This helps to reduce inefficiencies and ensure everyone has an equal opportunity to contribute to the organization.

Overall, inclusion and accessibility can help solve a range of problems in the workplace, from discrimination and bias to poor communication and inefficient processes. Organizations can foster a positive and productive work environment where everyone can thrive by creating a workplace culture that values diversity and promotes equity.

There are several ways to promote inclusion and accessibility in the workplace:

Create an inclusive culture: Creating an inclusive culture starts at the top. Leaders should model inclusive behavior, set clear expectations for employees, and prioritize diversity and equity in all aspects of the organization.

Training and education: Providing training and education on inclusion and accessibility can help employees understand why these values are important and how they can contribute to a more inclusive and accessible workplace. Provide accommodations for employees with disabilities or other needs to ensure everyone has an equal opportunity to participate in the workplace.

Foster open communication: Creating an environment of open communication and respect for different perspectives reduces misunderstandings and conflicts and foster collaboration.

Hire and promote diverse talent: Hiring and promoting individuals from diverse backgrounds and experiences creates a more diverse and inclusive workplace.

Review policies and practices: Reviewing policies and practices with an inclusion and accessibility lens can help identify areas where improvements can be made.

Measure and track progress: Measuring and tracking progress on inclusion and accessibility helps organizations identify areas for improvement and celebrate successes.

Promoting inclusion and accessibility in the workplace requires a commitment from leadership, a willingness to educate and train employees, and a dedication to creating an environment that values diversity and promotes equity.

Promoting inclusion and accessibility can help a business be more competitive in several ways:

Attracting and retaining top talent: When an organization prioritizes inclusion and accessibility, it creates a positive work environment that attracts top talent. Employees want to work for organizations that value diversity and equity and are more likely to stay with a company that provides an inclusive and accessible workplace.

Improving employee productivity and innovation: Inclusion and accessibility help employees feel more engaged and motivated, leading to increased productivity and innovation. When employees feel valued and supported, they are more likely to contribute their unique perspectives and ideas to help the organization succeed.

Expanding customer base: Customers increasingly want to do business with companies that share their values. By promoting inclusion and accessibility, organizations can attract and retain customers who prioritize these values.

Improving reputation: Inclusion and accessibility are increasingly important societal values. By promoting these values, organizations can improve their reputation and attract socially conscious investors, partners, and customers.

Overall, promoting inclusion and accessibility can help a business be more competitive by attracting and retaining top talent, improving employee productivity and innovation, expanding the customer base, mitigating legal risks, and improving reputation.

An organization can best embrace inclusion and accessibility by:

Developing a culture of inclusion: It's essential to develop a culture of inclusion where everyone feels welcome and valued. This includes promoting diversity, equity, and inclusion in all aspects of the organization, from recruitment and hiring, to training and development, to leadership and decision-making.

Conducting an accessibility audit: An accessibility audit can help identify areas where the organization can improve accessibility for employees, customers, and other stakeholders. This includes physical accessibility, digital accessibility, and accessibility in communication.

Training and education: It's crucial to provide training and education to employees, managers, and leaders on the importance of inclusion and accessibility. This includes training on unconscious bias, cultural competence, and disability awareness.

Providing accommodations: It's important to accommodate employees with disabilities or other needs to ensure they have an equal opportunity to participate in the workplace.

Reviewing policies and practices: It's essential to review policies and practices to ensure that they are inclusive and accessible. This includes recruitment, hiring, performance management, and employee benefits policies.

Encouraging open communication: It's important to encourage open communication and respect for different perspectives to create a more inclusive and collaborative work environment.

Measuring and tracking progress: It's important to measure and track progress on inclusion and accessibility to identify areas for improvement and celebrate successes.

By embracing inclusion and accessibility, organizations can create a positive and productive work environment where everyone can thrive. However, it requires a commitment from leadership, a willingness to educate and train employees, and a dedication to creating an environment that values diversity and promotes equity.

An organization can best leverage an inclusive and accessible workforce by:

Fostering a culture of innovation and collaboration: An inclusive and accessible workforce can bring diverse perspectives, ideas, and experiences to the table, leading to increased creativity and innovation. By fostering a culture of innovation and collaboration, organizations can leverage each employee's unique strengths to achieve their goals.

Providing training and development opportunities: Providing training and development opportunities can help employees build new skills and advance their careers, leading to increased engagement and retention. It's essential to offer training and development opportunities that are accessible to all employees, regardless of their background or abilities.

Encouraging employee engagement: Engaged employees are more productive and motivated, leading to better business outcomes. Therefore, it's essential to encourage employee engagement by providing feedback, recognition, and growth opportunities.

Promoting diversity and inclusion: Organizations can attract and retain top talent from diverse backgrounds and experiences by promoting diversity and inclusion. This can lead to a more inclusive and innovative workforce that is better equipped to meet the needs of customers and stakeholders.

Building strong employee networks: Employee networks can provide a sense of belonging and support for employees from diverse backgrounds. By building strong employee networks, organizations can foster a sense of community and promote inclusion and accessibility.

Measuring and tracking progress: It's important to measure and track progress on inclusion and accessibility to identify areas for improvement and celebrate successes. By regularly monitoring progress, organizations can ensure that they are leveraging their inclusive and accessible workforce to achieve their business goals.

An inclusive and accessible workforce can significantly benefit an organization, including increased innovation, productivity, and engagement. To leverage these benefits, organizations must foster a culture of inclusion, provide training and development opportunities, encourage employee engagement, promote diversity and inclusion, build strong employee networks, and measure and track progress.

It's human nature to pull away from something different from you. We like our tribes, and if you look at demographics in the US, you will see that people of the same ethnicity and culture tend to find one spot to live in because it's comfortable to be around people you know and trust and who are like you. I can't fault people for naturally migrating toward their people.

I don't think people are intentionally non-inclusive or racist or biased. I think that often, people are uneducated or have been raised a certain way with false narratives, which has shaped their beliefs about people. But as with many things in nature, nature adapts, and so do people. Once they realize different is not a threat, they usually can adapt to the situation or person.

Now, are there exceptions to these rules? Of course. Have you ever hung out with junior high girls? I call them the most vicious animal of all when it comes to not being inclusive. But if you look at the mental aspect, they are intimidated, insecure, and threatened. So how do they behave?

With that narrative, we can see why people behave as they do. But, again, this is not an excuse, just understanding the nature of things and then learning how we educate to change that narrative.

I have firsthand experience of what it's like to have a disability and be treated differently. For example, when I was in college, I was told by one professor, when I received a D on a paper, that I was not smart enough to be in college and should drop out. What was more shocking is that this professor was unwilling to help me learn how to improve.

I didn't fit his narrative of a college student, and so he didn't even want to consider whether I could learn how to be a better writer. Since he was an Ivy League professor, I thought a young girl from the country with little money didn't fit his narrative, and he was doing me a favor. Just as I thought I was doing a favor for the physically disabled people I was not hiring because I underestimated them.

I challenge you to continue to educate yourself and get comfortable with being uncomfortable.

About the Author

Dr. Julie Ducharme is a sought-after keynote speaker, author, business consultant, entrepreneur, instructor, and special consultant in women's empowerment. She is the creator, founder, and CEO of Julie's Party People, JD Consulting, Synergy Learning, and Taylor Elite Sports.

Navigating Change in Inclusive Leadership

Lynn Hoerauf

Inclusion means welcoming everyone, inviting everyone, and including everyone. Whether it be a business venture, school, or recreational activity, inclusion is where everyone has a sense of belonging and can freely engage, using their unique perspectives and strengths without fearing rejection.

Different people experience belonging differently, so it is our job as leaders to determine what inclusion is from their standpoint rather than basing it solely on our own experience. We change our mindsets as we become more open and aware of our unconscious biases.

Inclusion embraces people from all walks of life, celebrating their gifting and uniqueness without prejudging their contribution and potential. Accessibility looks at a situation—a building, process, or project—through a lens of openness that assures ease of use for potential stakeholders.

Inclusion and accessibility ensure that all potential clients or personnel users can be fully involved and invested in your organization. This is an opportunity for everyone to come forward as themselves, accepted for who they are. When people feel like they belong, they are free to offer more of themselves and are not concerned about making mistakes or coming off in a way that somebody could reject. This freedom of acceptance and belonging is at the heart of inclusion.

Inclusive and accessible qualities provide a welcoming environment that meets psychological, physical, and relational needs. So even though we are in an age of anxiety where just going into a workplace is difficult for some, when these needs are met, you will find a satisfied, fulfilled, and happier workplace and environment. This is huge. So many mental and physical challenges can be avoided when a workplace is inclusive and accessible. This kind of atmosphere radiates warmth and welcoming acknowledgment. It brings incredible benefits for those working or doing business at a job site where this sense of belonging and fulfillment occurs. It's an environment with five-star ratings and increased customer satisfaction.

As businesses grew more aware of the need for physical accessibility for their employees and customers, they saw the benefits of these changes for everyone. Improving accessibility meant adding ramps, automatic doors, or lights that turn on automatically without switches. In time, people realized that not only were these items essential for those with disabilities, but they also ended up helping everyone. For instance, if someone is trying to enter a building with their hands full of supplies, it is easier to push the automatic door opener than to set everything down and open it by hand. In the same way, adding automatic lights for those who have difficulty managing light switches saves electricity because they automatically turn off when no one is in the room. Thinking about the needs of others ultimately benefits everyone.

There is a concept called Universal Design that began in architecture and has gained popularity in the arenas of online education, web design, and workforce policy. It means things should be developed so the most people can access them under the greatest number of circumstances.

Universal Design came about as business owners realized it was cheaper to build their buildings with these adaptations already in the plans rather than retrofitting them later. Universal Design looks at a project from conception and determines the best course of action in the blueprint stage. Translating this to your business policy means that it's easier, in the long run, to put in the effort upfront to build in inclusion and accessibility than it is to come back later and try to fix a substandard policy.

Leadership is a challenge on its own. However, when leaders ensure that inclusion and accessibility are in place, they come in with the deck stacked. They are a step ahead when the needs of the employees and customers are met from the inclusion and accessibility standpoint. As a result, it is a smooth-running organization where employees have fewer hassles and more productivity because of inclusion and accessibility.

Many companies and businesses provide benefits above and beyond the norm because they know they will keep their employees longer if they provide for those servicing their company and customers. It provides cohesiveness and stability to the organization. When the time, effort, and finances that could be spent to re-hire and re-train are front-loaded into the areas of accessibility and inclusion, you keep your staff. Instead of re-training and re-hiring, this energy and money can be invested into increasing development and taking the company further.

Leaders are the glue that holds the organization and the team together. Leaders juggle differing personalities and make sure the job gets done. I will never forget this leader I worked with, who was this organization's rock. The staff had various perspectives and needs, but this leader met each person where they were. As a result, everyone felt valued and listened to. Each worker had a sense that this leader understood where they were coming from and what talents they brought to the organization, and they were treated with great respect and belonging. The staff worked well with their differing strengths, and sometimes they butted heads. However, I observed each person gave their all and felt invested in the company, and I think it was because they felt the leadership invested in them. They knew they mattered and that their opinions and work made a difference.

This was a cohesive unit, but there was a void when this leader took a new position. The shift in management changed the sense of inclusion and ease of use that each member previously experienced. As a result, the team became frustrated and turned on each other. Some left the organization, and unfortunately, what used to be a smooth-running operation became an ineffective unit. I learned a lot by watching this transpire, and I saw firsthand the value of inclusion and accessibility that had been previously in place under the former leader.

As briefly mentioned above, the social and psychological needs of the employee and customers are better met when inclusion and accessibility are in place. But, again, it's the idea of being prepared ahead of time. Pre-work or preparation allows for much more flexibility and advancement of a company or an idea. It's hard to say how many problems are avoided because this groundwork of creating a sense of inclusion and providing for needs to be met solves difficulties and glitches before they occur, making them a non-issue.

When inclusion and accessibility are built into the system, the groundwork exists for a positive and welcoming environment. When the leadership embraces this mindset to help one population of employees or customers, the benefits flow to others, and the entire environment improves.

I know of one leader who regularly dealt with a discontent employee, which caused both a lack of productivity and dissension in the team as team members were drawn into the drama of the situation and felt a need to take sides. Ultimately, the leader sought counsel for this issue from someone in another organization. The mentor shared that certain perspectives are held by those in the culture of the employee but not in the leader's culture. She realized that, even though she had the best intentions for the employee, by not understanding the employee's background and point of view, her approach was offensive rather than effective.

Armed with this new insight, she could approach the employee from a different angle and eventually earn back the employee's trust. This leader ultimately discovered that this new mindset improved her work relationships because it became a goal to understand her employees and work with them as individuals while appreciating their needs. Leaders set the tone for the organization. An important piece to this is being open to counsel and new ways of thinking and approaching the workplace.

An idea that could help to promote inclusion and accessibility in the workplace better is to ask those who are working there what they see. With the differing vantage points, workers and customers can offer unique solutions and ideas. So, find out what the people around you think, what they see, their opinion on how things work, and suggestions for improvement.

You could also have a brainstorming session during a meeting and lay it all out, discussing options together. Then, make it a game and have a competition where people can use their critical thinking skills, offer suggestions and ideas, and have fun doing it.

It's amazing how our brains work differently, and our perspectives see differently. And although not every idea may be effective, gathering more information and allowing for opportunities for insight can bring across thoughts that successfully support inclusion and accessibility in a way not otherwise considered.

There is always the option of putting together a committee to focus on these areas. This would allow those passionate about making these areas shine in your organization to use their skills and insights to promote a more positive work environment. As you have probably already noticed, many organizations are creating offices to enhance diversity, equity, inclusion, and accessibility. Focusing on these essential areas, they develop ways to organize, advocate, and stimulate the workplace.

With so many job openings and unemployment rates remaining fairly low, many organizations are hiring, and those looking to change their employment have the advantage. We spend so much of our lives working, and since COVID, many have made adjustments by re-prioritizing their work life. Individuals have not only reset their values but also set an intention to enjoy more of their life, including their work. They want to draw the most they can from their time, and even the term "work-life balance" has made its way into everyday conversation. By offering a workplace centered on a sense of belonging and meeting the needs of workers through accessibility, you will draw people who want to work in your organization.

As we know, having the choice of employees gives the employer the advantage of choosing those who would match our available positions. It also increases our competitiveness by operating with top-notch personnel. People want to work where they enjoy working and stay where they enjoy working. These two areas alone increase our ability to have a successful operation. Our efforts and finances can go into the organization, and we can focus on improving rather than replacing our staff.

This kind of reputation—where people feel safe, important, and satisfied—becomes common knowledge and continues to draw the best of the best.

No matter where you are on your journey, reading this book and others on the topic will help you embrace inclusion and accessibility. So, great work! You are taking steps in the right direction by filling your mind with ideas and insights to help you make new choices and implement new practices to help your organization embrace inclusion and accessibility better.

We adopt and incorporate ideologies more easily when we see their importance. Sometimes it could be that we realize what we are doing—or what we aren't doing—is causing us to go in a direction we don't want to be going in. That's the time when we reassess and make new resolutions. Continue to seek support and information to integrate the principles of inclusion and accessibility successfully.

Having a day away retreat or regular sessions helps penetrate the current corporate culture, but it can also highlight and celebrate effective and thriving areas. So many people and organizations are doing great things. Featuring these successes offers positive morale and boosts employee confidence, helping them know they are working in the right place.

Acceptance begets acceptance. As the leaders of an organization move toward a more inclusive and accessible environment, the organization's culture changes. As the atmosphere changes, the employees' mindsets shift. Openness takes the place of fear, and acceptance replaces bias. A fundamental change in the beliefs of the leadership will translate into a change in those they lead.

As this happens, the team members become part of the movement toward a more accepting and understanding workplace. The employees become the agents of change and help ensure that others experience a welcoming environment and are more likely to stay in their positions long-term. This same spirit translates to their work with your clients. This means those who already use your services will most likely use them more, but you will draw new clients looking for the atmosphere you bring.

Changing an organization's culture can't be done by the leadership alone. It may need to start there, but the more you can involve your team in transitioning to an inclusive and accessible organization, the better.

Sometimes we can become anxious or unsure about how to incorporate ideas or that we need to catch up to the times more than we wish. Be sure to take a moment to recognize the positives that you and your company are already doing in the areas of inclusion and accessibility. Start with your strengths. What has helped your company become a place where people want to work? How is your company already taking part in being inclusive and accessible? This may be a time to celebrate the areas already in place.

Upon some reflection, this is when you want to do an overhaul and go to the ground level to restructure. Gather some resources and make a strategy. In this time of rebuilding, you can feel a new excitement about what is coming.

Get input from your staff and tweak some areas. Maybe it's time to put a counsel in place to lead the reorganizing efforts. But, again, this is an exciting way to expand and improve your already productive and positive efforts.

Most leaders I have met have the best intentions to assist their staff in being the best versions of themselves and to help their company meet the needs and desires of consumers and stakeholders. Whatever it is, give yourself time, continue to seek best practices, and share this book series and other informational sources with others. Then, take it on as a mission to continue doing great things for your company, employees, and clients.

ABOUT THE AUTHOR

Lynn M. Hoerauf is a speaker and award-winning author of the Rom-Com *Miss Snickers*. She enjoys sharing humor and insight while cheering people on as they flourish in their lives, work, and relationships. For more information, tune into her Relational Effectiveness podcast on the Strategic Advisor Board channel or go to LynnSpeaks.com.

A Sense of Belonging and the Right Tools

Ryan Jackson and Brianna Jackson

Inclusion means everyone in an organization feels like they have a place and what they contribute is recognized and valued. An inclusive organization means the organization acknowledges, appreciates, and uses the unique viewpoints, talents, and skills of members of all backgrounds.

"Accessibility is the design, construction, development and maintenance of facilities, information and communication technology, programs, and services so that all people, including people with disabilities, can fully and independently use them."

–Nikita M. Floore, "Diversity, Equity, Inclusion and Accessibility: A Foundation for Meaningful Change," United States Department of Labor Blog

Accessibility is about providing the tools and resources that are required to establish and maintain a base level of opportunity for productivity for each individual. It is up to each individual to perform to their desired output level, but the key is that there is an inclusive and accessible starting point. We often use the term "issue" to describe diversity, equity, and inclusion challenges, but that doesn't imply a problem. Every human being is different. Don't think about this as just a "people with special needs" issue. Instead, establish the mindset that everyone has their own unique circumstances. You don't have to be on the extreme end of a spectrum to need improved accessibility and inclusion. These attributes are just as crucial for the ordinary people in the middle.

When many people think of accessibility, they often think only of handicaps. However, it's not just about handicaps. It can be those big things, like having a ramp into your building or an elevator for people in a wheelchair, but it's also for those who just got done with surgery because life happens, and our bodies don't always function the way they did previously. So we go to the doctor and have some work done, and then we have to do some physical therapy. Sometimes, we need additional support. That is also accessibility.

Inclusion is also about not treating someone differently because they need extra support or tools or come from a different background or circumstances. If you observe most young children, you will see a ton of inclusion. Young children have not yet been shaped to have biases or preferences in who they pick to sit by or play with, especially when put in a new environment. When you come back to the same group, you will see they have developed their trends based on their interactions and whether they got what they wanted. Now you will see them give preferential treatment or avoid "the biter" as an example.

As adults, we have been quietly molding ourselves our whole life and our conscious and unconscious biases sometimes drive our interactions. Understanding how that plays out can help us ensure we are not exclusive of others from the onset. Ultimately, most people just want to feel like they are a part of something. If we approach new environments more like curious children, open to everyone in the group, we can help foster inclusion in our organizations and lives.

Inclusion and accessibility are the tools to ensure an organization is truly diverse and equitable with equal opportunities. Accessibility is critical in team members performing their duties to the best of their abilities and capabilities. Inclusion means an organization actively recognizes the efforts, outputs, and results of all members. Succeeding in being a highly accessible workplace is pointless if an organization doesn't correctly include all of those within the workplace. It is not logical and it is bad business to invest resources in accessibility and then not capitalize on the returns from that investment.

We can dive a little deeper into accessibility with the following example. Remember the days of paper tests when you sat there with your sealed booklet and your number two pencil. When the instructor was ready for you to start, you were directed to take the number two pencil and break the seal of the test booklet. The seal was a little piece of tape, and like opening a letter, you would run the pencil underneath it and use that to rip open the seal.

Now, imagine that you're sitting in this room full of other test takers, and you look around everybody has their booklet, and everybody has their number two pencil, but you look down at your desk and all you have is the booklet, you don't have a number two pencil. What do you do? You raise your hand and ask for a pencil, but the instructor is busy giving directions and walking around, checking to make sure nobody has notes written on their hands. The instructor is ignoring you. So you just sit there with your booklet and no number two pencil. Now you have a pen in your bag right next to you. But you're not allowed to use a pen on these tests because they require a number two pencil so the scoring machine can grade them. The machine will only pick up marks made by a number two pencil. So you are not going to be able to complete your test. You are failing and you didn't have the access to the right tools to even begin.

This is what it feels like for many people. When there's not good accessibility as part of an organization's inclusion and diversity dynamics, it feels like sitting in the testing room without your number two pencil. It is critical to every organization to ensure the right balance of accessibility exists for each individual within your organization so they can be productive. Without the right tools, they fail before they can even begin, and in addition to the hits on your productivity, it is demoralizing.

So now that everyone has the right tools, and the test is accessible, what if we consider that the group includes individuals whose dominant language is not English? If the test is written only in English, several people may not feel like the test offers a very inclusive environment for them. However, if you had tests available in multiple languages or translation support, you could improve both accessibility and the people's feelings of inclusion, which then not only allows them to perform the test but to perform it in a more positive mental state. When people feel supported, they are more likely to perform to their best potential and that is part of what makes these issues so important for organizations to recognize.

Inclusion and accessibility encompass all the tools a leader must use to implement diversity and equity while ensuring equal opportunities. At the macro level for inclusion, it means leaders ensure everyone has a place at the table. Make sure everyone has the opportunity to provide input or effort, recognize the value of their input or effort, and encourage others to do the same via constructive discussion about the input and effort. It is important to reprimand non-constructive discussion in real time without dismissing the sources of that non-constructive discussion. However, an open and honest discussion in private with the people providing non-constructive input needs to be addressed later to make those individuals aware of the negative effects of their methods. You can then educate them on providing more positive impacts and effects in future interactions. By doing this, leaders will make their teams more efficient and effective, providing better results and productivity.

To implement accessibility, it is important to ensure the resources to achieve equity are properly implemented and to achieve "follow through." A leader most likely cannot personally implement all the resources needed to achieve equity. However, a leader needs to ensure those responsible for the implementation are held accountable for ensuring all team members have access to the resources, regardless of their unique circumstances.

A personal example of a lack of accessibility that I unfortunately experienced regularly in the military was when the workload on members of an organization was not equal. This often resulted in the members of an organization with a lighter workload being able to focus on personal growth, such as professional education, undergraduate and graduate degrees, certifications, etc. In comparison, the members with a heavier workload did not have the excess time to focus on personal growth without sacrificing their time with family, community service, or passions. Eventually, this can result in an inequitable situation that impacts the evaluation of service members. While two individuals may be doing their job, one is excelling at personal development because their workload allows it. When you rank two individuals objectively who both do their jobs well, the norm is to turn to who is going "above and beyond" in personal growth. Both individuals could be spending equal amounts of time and effort to excel, but both may not be able to focus on multiple areas of focus due to an imbalance.

Leaders must recognize the individual needs of their team to ensure they feel included. What if you have a team member who is much shorter than everyone else, and in your workspace, everyone has to be able to reach things higher up? If the majority of the team is tall enough to reach those items, it can be easy to overlook the one team member who can't reach or to assume others will help them. In that situation, the shorter individual does not have access to independently accomplish their work. They may feel like a burden to other team members, and the other members may also resent the shorter person for not being able to accomplish such a simple task. This lack of accessibility erodes the inclusion of your team.

As a leader, it is critical to look at the situation and provide the necessary tools. In this example, the small adjustment of providing the team with a stepstool can help equalize the accessibility for the shorter team member. It also makes it easier for taller team members, who may also choose to use the stepstool even though they didn't initially understand why it was needed. When something does not directly impact you, it is easy to overlook it. However, leaders are charged with paying attention to those details for their teams to grow and thrive. This small adjustment vastly improves the independence and feeling of being cared for and included.

There are two issues to note in this example as well. The first issue is what you, as a leader, are doing to recognize what access is needed by the people on your team. The second issue touches much more directly on whether you have built an inclusive environment. For example, does the shorter individual speak up and ask for the stepstool or are they hesitant? Have you built an organization that promotes equity and inclusion? Are individuals with differences comfortable asking for extra support? Is your culture one that proclaims, *I'm willing to help you do the best job that you can do*, or does your organization have barriers making it difficult to get support or feel bad for asking for a tool or a resource? This difference is important to understand. If you're in charge of the organization, recognizing what climate and dynamic you have set, or allowed passively, is the key to building a more inclusive and accessible future.

Inclusion and accessibility are important to implementing diversity, equity, and equal opportunities. Therefore, all the problems discussed in the two previous books in this series—*Business Leadership and Diversity* and *Business Leadership and Equity*—that can be solved by diversity and equity are also solved by proper inclusion and accessibility.

Teams in a workplace can be thrown off when there is an imbalance in resources or when individual members don't feel included. It erodes morale and productivity and eventually breeds resentment or hostile workplace issues. However, by focusing on inclusion and accessibility, organizations and their leaders can proactively tackle the onset symptoms of these issues before they evolve into anything larger. So, having solid and legitimate policies and culture for inclusion and accessibility can deter many of the negative issues faced in business.

All members of an organization can be servant leaders and implement the tools and methods that a positional leader has identified within the organization. Do not wait for the solution, be the solution. Ensure that people are educated, trained, and held accountable for implementing inclusion and accessibility. All levels and initiatives of an organization should have a standard practice of addressing and assessing the implementation of inclusion and accessibility.

Are you open and supportive of everybody on your team? Are you recognizing or seeing that your people ask for things when they need them? If not, look at your accessibility policies, the processes supporting it, and how your business operates. You can then make sure you don't have any barriers, even passive or unconscious barriers, to people getting everything they need to be successful for you to reap the benefits of your team and for individuals to feel like included members.

You need everyone on your team to be successful. And if they can't be successful without certain tools, then it's your job as a leader to ensure they have access to them. The organization must demonstrate its willingness to be supportive, whether the tools are immediately apparent or available. Does your organization have in place what it needs to provide accessibility? Do you have the right resources? It's as simple as whether you have a number two pencil or enough number two pencils for everybody on the team to be successful. It also goes back to some of the policies. Do you have the right policies in place to support providing resources and tools as they are needed? Do you have the right policies to promote people asking for resources for you to identify what is required? It's two-fold in that people have to be willing to ask, but you have to set the environment that supports and encourages that ask.

Knowing what it is that your people might need and proactively ensuring that you can get a hold of those resources are the things that will help keep your organization on the front edge of the accessibility and inclusion issues.

An inclusive and accessible organization is the difference between claiming to be diverse and equitable based on statistics and metrics and ensuring your people feel included as a diverse group and can use the resources provided to them to achieve equity. By truly achieving diversity and equity when the vast majority of members feel that the organization is in that state, members will be more committed, productive, happy, and healthy. This results in reduced costs associated with members in a negative state of mind and body, and an increase in revenue due to the members being in a positive state of mind and body.

If you're doing the same thing everybody else does, competition boils down to who's cheaper. It comes down to price versus return, but not everything should always be about price. Instead, you want to get people focused on the quality of why what you're offering is the best, and why what you're offering will meet the need better than anything else. The only way you can find that value proposition is by having a diverse team with diverse skills and perspectives helping you develop those pitches. That team then needs the right culture and tools to ensure their production reaches that level.

Inclusion and accessibility need to be embraced the same as diversity and equity. All four of these need to be part of a comprehensive program by an organization to educate, inform, stimulate open conversation, clearly defined objectives, and frequent assessment through non-attributable means. This gives the organization a good idea of where they started, where they are going, how they are getting there, and what their destination is.

You can't send somebody in a wheelchair to a bike race without a hand bike, right? They can't use a foot-pedal-driven bike;

they need to use a hand-crank-driven bike. This does not mean they cannot compete in the race. It means we need to give them the right tools for the race to ensure that they have the opportunity to be successful. And that's what accessibility is all about. It's about having the right tools. It's having the right policies.

So let's talk about the policy piece for just a minute. If you look beyond just ensuring accessible tools and resources and look at the accessibility of growth opportunities, then what are the paths of your opportunities? What are the paths of your additional work certifications? And who has access to those paths? Thirty years ago, many organizations operated under a kind of growth-from-within model. You start as a salesperson in a corporation and then you might become the manager of that department. As you climb the promotion ladder, you may manage multiple floors or departments. And then maybe you become a store director and then maybe you get onto the board of the company that owns the store. There was a pretty well recognized ladder approach to how you climbed toward success. The promotion path was well defined.

In today's world, that's not how the workforce operates anymore. There are still some ladders within organizations, but more often what you see are lateral moves. People go from one set of organizations to another, often for a new experience. The driver is less about promotion and more about learning a new nuance of how they apply their skill sets. For example, if they've always applied their skill sets in clothing, they might try to apply their skill sets in medical supplies. Although it's a completely different industry, with a different set of rules, the opportunity to expand the depth of their skill sets is most appealing. The key to retaining talent is to look for ways to make that kind of cross training accessible within your organization. Maximizing opportunities for team members to grow their skills is part of making them feel valued and included.

When you look at accessibility, you want to look across your entire organization from your CEO to your newest salesperson and identify the available opportunities. Sometimes that's overlooked, and sometimes the paths to your organization's different aspects are only visible in one department. Maybe one department is great at advertising all the paths within the company or even just one of these specific great certification opportunities, but the other departments may not advertise it as well, so their people are not exposed to it. It's not accessible to them.

If you do that and ensure you have a fair marketing of those different opportunities, you'll find the more accessible you make those opportunities, the more qualified and diverse candidates you will see for those programs. That's what we've been driving to demonstrate ways you can grow diversity.

This may lead you to ask, "How do you promote diversity?" and "How do you leverage diversity?" If you only recruit people from one part of your organization to apply for your programs, and those people all come with a similar background and skills, you will stovepipe yourself into groupthink, a singular direction, one path. But if you expand the accessibility of the programs to your greater organization, you will then pull from a wider variety of different skills sets. The team that you can build in those programs is going to be much more unique, much more creative, much more diverse, which is what helps companies achieve a competitive edge. Opening up and making more accessible all the opportunities that you have in your organization is a key piece to driving productivity and results.

How we have described it may sound like you must be a big organization to do all these things. But that's not true. You can do this in smaller organizations as well. Small businesses can promote accessibility for tools and resources as well as cross training opportunities for individual skill set growth as well. It may not be as broadly focused as the example we described with internal certification paths and internal programs. Those tend to be more robust in larger businesses, but you can apply the same principles of just looking at how you hire, for example. Where do you advertise jobs? Where do you post? Are you posting your advertisements in diverse enough groupings and pages to ensure that it's accessible to a wider pool of candidates? How inclusive are you in where you seek candidates? Do you visit new places to look for new hires or only the same old spots?

This doesn't imply that you need to change any of the qualifications for your job. You need to have people qualified, with the right skill sets. That's important. Don't change that. But maybe change where you're advertising because you may think, *I just need to advertise here because this is where this candidate pool lives.* But I encourage you to also throw it out to a couple of other random places you might not think of as a prospective candidate pool because you might just find some diamonds in the rough. You might just find some additional talent that everyone else has overlooked. And when you find that talent that's been overlooked, that's also where you find a competitive edge.

When an organization succeeds in being inclusive, you will be able to recognize the strengths of your members. This will allow you to build teams around their strengths, personalities, and characteristics. You will achieve higher results when you build teams with good dynamics and balanced strengths. This will result in a better product or service for your customers.

Now, once you bring all those teams together, you can return to the number two pencil example. Start by ensuring that everyone on your team has everything they need to do the work you're asking of them. Make sure that it's accessible to them. For them to be productive, they have to be able to have the tools and the resources to produce.

Especially look at your own internal diversity, equity, and inclusion programs. Are those accessible for success? Are they going to achieve the results that you want them to achieve? What are they doing and what tools and resources have you given them to deep dive into your organization and your team members to make a difference or impact? What goals have you given them to strive for to promote real change from within? If those groups are poorly organized and equipped, what kind of message are you sending to your organization? You have met face value, but most individuals long for a deeper connection. A true sense of inclusion. Being a productive part of the team with accessibility to the right tools and growth opportunities to promote their independent development.

If your DEI programs are not resourced well, why do you have them? People may not necessarily find that insulting but probably a little condescending. You have an organization, and you say it's going to promote these things, but then you've given it no guidance, no resources, and the people you've put in charge of it are probably the most outwardly diverse person from the team. You stereotyped them and put them in charge because they look like a diverse individual, which isn't necessarily fair to that individual. That may or may not be their skill set. Although they may be able to adapt, if you haven't given them strategic vision and you haven't given them tools or resources, then you haven't made that job accessible for them to be successful. And that's what's important.

To maximize the inclusivity of your organization, you have to make sure that everybody has that equal playing field, that all the tools and resources are accessible to everyone on the team. That is how you're going to drive inclusion. That is how you're going to drive productivity and that is how you're going to drive your products or services. That is how you are an inclusive and accessible organization in truth, not just numbers on paper.

If you need a partner (or team member) who takes an organization's best interest to establish a comprehensive diversity and equity initiative with proper inclusion and accessibility to implement your initiative, please contact Sonas at sonasclan.com.

ABOUT THE AUTHOR

Brianna Jackson, founder and CEO of Sonas, is a master at developing strategic frameworks that take an organization to the next level. A mother of four boys with 20 years of leadership and management experience in the federal government, she knows how to manage resources, build and empower teams, tackle the most daunting problem sets, and realize the maximum potential and profits for any industry.

* * *

Ryan Jackson retired from the U.S. Navy after 24 years of service within the enlisted and officer ranks. He is currently a small business owner and pursing various entrepreneurial ventures.

Ryan Jackson
President
Valhalla Properties, LLC

Lessons from the Army to the Workplace

Mike Jackson

Inclusion and accessibility hold a special place in my heart, and I've witnessed firsthand the tremendous progress society has made in these areas. When I was younger, my mother injured her back, and seeing the positive changes that have been made since then fills me with hope. It's incredible how far we've come in making the world more accessible for everyone.

During my nearly 27-year career in the US Army, I had many incredible experiences. However, those years also took a toll on my body. Multiple injuries sustained, both in training and on combat deployments, have left me with a few disabilities, such as significant hearing loss.

Although I'm nearly deaf in one ear and have only about 30% hearing in the other, I'm grateful for the strides made in hearing aid technology. While it's not perfect and can't help me in every situation, it's still remarkable how organizations have adapted to accommodate those of us with hearing impairments. This is just one example of how modern society has embraced inclusion and accessibility.

In addition to my challenges, I've seen my brothers-in-arms face their own struggles. Many have lost limbs, but prosthetic technology has advanced by leaps and bounds. These advancements, spurred in part by the needs of injured service members during the Global War on Terror, have enabled them to regain mobility and independence.

In short, I am deeply appreciative of the progress society has made in promoting inclusion and accessibility. By sharing these personal stories, I hope to inspire others to continue pushing for a world that welcomes everyone, regardless of their abilities.

Inclusion and accessibility play a crucial role in today's workplace, particularly given the sizable number of employees with disabilities. The Centers for Disease Control and Prevention report that about 25% of the US population in communities has some form of disability. Similarly, over a billion people worldwide are affected by disabilities. It's clear that without a solid inclusion and accessibility plan in place, workplaces risk isolating a significant portion of potential talent.

From a purely business perspective, it's a no-brainer. What company would want to eliminate 25% of their prospective employee pool, especially in today's competitive job market?

Embracing inclusion and accessibility is not only ethically sound but also an intelligent business strategy.

Throughout my career in the US Army, I experienced firsthand the power of inclusion and accessibility in the workplace. The Army, and the US Government as a whole, have clear policies to ensure these values are upheld. I recall when the Army's motto was "An Army of One." It's hard to imagine a better way to encapsulate the essence of inclusion and accessibility. Every soldier and service member collaborate towards a common goal, united as one.

This sense of unity resonates deeply with the founding principles of the United States of America—that we are one nation, stronger together than we are individually. By embracing inclusion and accessibility, we honor this ideal and create a more inclusive society for everyone.

As a leader, it's essential to ask yourself: why would you ever want to exclude or make parts of your workplace inaccessible to your employees or customers? Frankly, it doesn't make sense. I recognize that for some small businesses, implementing accessibility accommodations simultaneously could be financially challenging. In these cases, leaders must collaborate with the employees in question to develop a phased plan that won't overburden the company while working towards comprehensive inclusion and accessibility.

Involving employees in determining the priorities for implementing an inclusion and accessibility plan is a significant step in the right direction. Taking their suggestions on board demonstrates a genuine commitment to creating a more accessible and supportive environment.

One of the core principles I learned as a soldier was the value of people in achieving a mission. When you care for your people, they'll ensure the mission is accomplished correctly and efficiently. Part of taking care of your team involves providing them with everything they need to excel in their roles, and that's where inclusion and accessibility come into play. By embracing these values, you empower your employees, foster a more inclusive work environment, and ultimately, drive your organization's success.

Inclusion and accessibility in the workplace are critical in fostering unity among employees and coworkers. When there's a lack of unity, fissures can develop between team members, and over time, these divisions may only grow larger. Often, these fissures can stem from seemingly minor issues that, if left unaddressed, can lead to more significant problems.

Take, for instance, a hearing-impaired employee who needs a specific accommodation to perform their job as effectively as their non-hearing-impaired colleagues. Without this accommodation, other employees might be perceived as better at their jobs, potentially creating a divide between team members. This fissure can be easily resolved by providing the necessary accommodation for the hearing-impaired employee.

Of course, not all issues related to inclusion and accessibility can be solved simply, but the underlying principle remains the same. By making an effort and devising a robust plan, leaders can promote unity among coworkers and ensure everyone feels valued and on an equal footing, regardless of their disabilities. In doing so, they create a more inclusive, harmonious, and productive work environment for all.

The old Army motto, "lead by example," is particularly relevant when fostering inclusion and accessibility in the workplace. When leaders demonstrate these values, they achieve several important goals. First, they set the standard for acceptable behavior, and second, they make enforcing these expectations among employees easier.

It's also crucial to have clear company policies outlining the consequences for employees who don't treat their colleagues equally, particularly in cases involving disabilities. While each company may handle these situations differently, I believe in a progressive approach to discipline. If the issue persists, an employee who mistreats a coworker should receive a verbal warning, followed by a written warning. If the same incident occurs a third time, dismissal from the company would be warranted.

Maintaining good order and discipline within a company is essential for efficient operations, and as a leader, it's part of your responsibility to address any issues that arise. Being proactive and having a plan for dealing with such situations is far better than finding yourself unprepared in a conflict. In addition, leading by example and implementing a solid plan will create a more inclusive and harmonious work environment for everyone.

When a company fully embraces inclusion and accessibility for all employees, there's a strong likelihood that it will operate more efficiently and productively. Efficiency and productivity are critical factors in determining a company's competitiveness within its industry. Conversely, if a company isn't running smoothly and lacks unity among its workforce, its chances of staying competitive are slim.

Unity is essential for bringing employees together and creating a cohesive team. A divided company is destined to fail eventually. However, when employees can rely on one another professionally and sometimes even personally, they become an unstoppable force.

By prioritizing inclusion and accessibility, you'll cultivate a sense of unity within your organization, paving the way for increased efficiency, productivity, and competitiveness. In addition, investing in an inclusive work environment leads to a more successful and resilient company.

As entrepreneurs, we've all realized that every employee is unique. There's no right or wrong type of employee, just different individuals with their own strengths and weaknesses. This understanding goes beyond the distinction between employees with and without disabilities.

Consider Merriam-Webster's online definition of disability: "a physical, mental, cognitive, or developmental condition that impairs, interferes with, or limits a person's ability to engage in certain tasks or actions or participate in typical daily activities and interactions." While not everyone has a disability, this definition leaves room for interpretation. For example, is a fear of the dark a disability? Of course, it could be, but only in certain situations. Similarly, a hearing-impaired person's disability only affects them when sound is necessary for their job.

Speaking from personal experience, I wasn't a fan of heights during my time in the Army. Nevertheless, I completed tasks at high altitudes, like military parachute jumps and rappelling. Now that I'm no longer required to perform such activities, I avoid high-altitude situations. My point is not to diminish anyone's disability but to emphasize that there's no such thing as a "normal" person. We all have our quirks and limitations.

So why not embrace each other's quirks and disabilities, treating everyone with the same respect and consideration we'd like to receive ourselves? I firmly believe in the Golden Rule, which has served me well so far. Of course, if I ever encounter a situation that doesn't apply, I'll reconsider my stance. But until then, I'll continue to treat others as I'd like to be treated.

Every employee comes with their own set of strengths and weaknesses. As a leader, it's essential to assess your team members to understand their preferences, needs, and capabilities. For example, someone may be trained in a specific area, but they might not enjoy the work.

Take my brother, for instance. He's a computer whiz, particularly in networking. But at this stage, he's lost interest in working with computers. I remember our conversation while he was casually resetting 600 passwords because a firewall was down. Unlike me, who struggled to organize my passwords, he could multitask effortlessly.

The takeaway is that employees are more likely to excel when they enjoy their work. If they're unhappy, their performance may suffer. As a leader, it's crucial to help your team members find roles that align with their interests and strengths. By doing so, you might be pleasantly surprised by the improvements in their performance and overall job satisfaction.

To wrap things up, fostering a workplace culture where employees follow the Golden Rule and treat one another with respect, regardless of their differences or disabilities, is essential. Help your team members find roles they're passionate about to maximize their effectiveness and productivity. Talent management is a crucial skill for leaders at all levels.

By promoting inclusion and accessibility within your company, you create opportunities for the best candidates to join your team, no matter their circumstances. As a leader, always set an excellent example for your employees. Doing so gives them a target to strive for and establishes the minimum standard of professionalism expected in the company.

Ultimately, the goal is to ensure your employees behave compassionately. By fostering a supportive and inclusive environment, you'll be amazed by what your team can achieve. The sky's the limit!

About the Author

Mike Jackson's experience includes developing and implementing policies and procedures, enforcing leadership standards, and assisting clients in implementing quality programs. He is also a regular facilitator and guest speaker at national and international healthcare conferences. He also consults for the Department of Defense, where he is one of the senior advisors to the Special Operations community on all things medical.

Breaking Down Invisible Barriers for a Better Workplace

Michael Markiewicz

S ome barriers and walls may be invisible to the eye, whether spoken or not. Diversity and inclusion mean the fall of the walls and barriers where everyone has the same opportunities.

The right experience and talent come in many colors, shapes and sizes, religions, ethnic groups, sexual orientations, and genders. The workplace may lose out on the best talent available if there are barriers around those identifiers.

If I were a leader of a particular organization, I would want the best talent available for me, my team, and the organization to be their best.

Many problems can be solved by inclusion and accessibility. Think of it like this, if any individual has the solution to a problem, but there is a barrier to entry based on some form of discrimination, then the problem will take a lot longer to solve and could cost a lot more money.

We can better promote inclusion and accessibility in the workplace by ensuring everyone has the same access. Someone's ethnic origin or what they believe in or look like should have no bearing on the task. What matters are knowledge, experience, and expertise. And that comes from anyone and anywhere. We promote it by ensuring the organization has a DEI program in place.

If the right knowledge, experience, and expertise exist, grab the person with those attributes, regardless of other factors. Incorporating DEI into the organization makes it more competitive against organizations that do not promote DEI. The more the organization is based on abilities, the more competitive it is.

Embrace DEI because you never know where your next solution will come from. Sometimes, people wear blinders based on some learned behavior based on a belief system that blinds them to where the real talent lies. My parting words are to take off the blinders and do yourself a favor by opening your team and organization to solutions based on experience and expertise, regardless of any other physical or belief system attributes they may have.

About the Author

Michael Markiewicz has over 30 years of experience in financial guidance, serving entertainment professionals, family offices, small businesses, and high net worth individuals. Previously, he held positions at CBIZ MHM Family Office Services, Deloitte & Touche, Marks Paneth & Shron, The Boston Company, and as the vice president and CFO of a private family office.

The Art of Advocacy: Empowering Ambassadorship in Your Sphere of Influence

Jessica M. Powers

My story begins on a cloudy March afternoon in a New England NIC unit. I was wheeled into my mom's room so she could see me for the first time, and she responded with shock. I was not what she expected when she committed to continuing the pregnancy. She needed time to process the complicated feelings to accept me in real life, as she did on bed rest in her prayers, believing whatever God gave her was perfect.

Weeks prior, my parents were told I would never walk, talk, see, or function like a healthy baby. I would not make it to my first birthday, and if I did survive, I would only be a vegetable to society and a burden to them to care for. They strongly encouraged an abortion to spare the necessary challenges they confidently predicted and said my parents should just try again for another healthy baby. I was not a living being with a heartbeat; I was invisible.

After an emergency C-section, the best-case scenario actually happened! We both survived the complications, but the fight was not over. I was born over three months premature, weighing one pound, four ounces, the smallest baby to survive at that time. I was so tiny that I wore doll clothes, and a funeral dress had been made for me in case I didn't make it. I stayed in the incubator for four months and graduated to breathing on my own.

You can imagine the medical bills and the trauma that colored this experience. That time of the pregnancy journey is when all the sensory nerves get developed, and there I was, exposed to a world of loud, bright constant chaos in the hospital, too fragile to hold with transparent skin.

Born to an English/art major and a mechanical engineer who met during their drum corps days, I had parents who were willing to advocate for me no matter what happened.

Miraculously, despite all the predictions, my vision was the only function compromised with a variation of ROP, a retina-related condition that required surgery and damaged my nerves from the high oxygen levels meant I needed custom prescription glasses. With no surprise, I gravitated toward artistic promise early on through writing and drawing on the back of those old-school white and green striped reams of paper my dad would bring home from work. The scraps of unintelligible printed code data on one side and endless drawing potential on the other. What more could I ask for?

A few of the proudest and most expressed moments of my life were winning ribbons at juried art competitions, learning to play the trumpet as a nod to my parents' marching band roots, passing my driving test on the first try, and obtaining a college degree—all things that were never supposed to be possible for a girl who was expected to be a vegetable.

This brief introduction paints the picture of my professional influence in our current world and why I care so deeply about the power of being an advocate. Who better to champion accelerator programs, incubator think tanks with some of the brightest minds in the world, and curate an embracive culture than someone who was in one?

As we discuss accessibility and inclusion, I point to my artistic roots and what I know, growing up in a sign shop with paint fumes, wood workshops, and a strong work ethic to prove viability from an industrial town with hard-working parents. It was important to prove value and worth through what we did. Our identity and sense of significance were framed by what we created with our hands, the precise accuracy we could see with our eyes, and what we could access for supplies.

I soon learned that I also lived in a world of bias that was not always safe to be expressive and transparent. There were not many neuro-diverse paths to follow. Mental health was not something openly discussed. I was bullied in school for being different and felt constantly compared to the expectation of being perfect and "normal" like everyone else. I learned to try to fit in to keep a low profile to protect myself from the embarrassment of any unwanted attention or needing more support with extra accommodations. I did not want to be a burden or be reminded of the pain I felt of being misunderstood.

This landscape was not easy to understand or accept, and I found myself unfairly let go of employment opportunities because I was not fast enough to do the visual tasks. Discrimination was real, and managers and HR departments knew how to bend the protocol and legal conversations to say it was for something other than visual impairment, even though they knew I was impaired when they hired me. It was painful and frustrating, especially because one of these companies was a well-known retail organization that prides itself on empowering people with disabilities and challenges.

This lived experience is the primer for creating more genuine awareness than assumptions, judgments, and profit over people that still coats the capitalistic culture we have in America. The exclusion of a whole demographic of creative talent that would be a huge asset to society, if they were no longer invisible, denied access, stripped of a voice, and were given more dignity with an honest conversation around where they would be better suited, whether than seen as a liability.

My heart for creating a richer experience of inclusion was recalibrated even more when I experienced a trio of events that pushed me back into a space of invisibility. But they became the catalyst for my newfound position in the marketplace to model even greater relevance to the importance of DEIA leadership.

In 2020, I started losing more of my vision with a surprise diagnosis related to my medical history. I suddenly had to learn to adapt to a new way of being in an unprepared world. Without seamless access to the tools and support around navigating vision loss and not qualifying for blind disability programs, I was devastated with grief, feeling dispensable because I felt my pace with vision loss was discrediting to my skill sets in some way. The hardest part was feeling I knew how to express and communicate with the world was also compromised.

Everything I did depended on this sense, and now life felt disorienting, with more sensory inputs to adjust to. I felt like I was also losing my vibrancy, voice, and value in the noise while becoming instantly more vulnerable. Being invisible became a safety net and superpower to fly under the radar. I began to understand there was an entire demographic in this exact limbo space in our society right now. They were people between two worlds, where I found an entire community experiencing the same sense of grief, insecurity, and questions about value in the marketplace.

I began to encounter other talented people in the shadows with so much to offer the world if they only had the opportunity to be visible and have their voices heard. The invisible ones like me are between folks who understand being in limbo with a diagnosis or event beyond their control. Most visually impaired or people with disabilities are not born this way. A small percentage of cane, braille, and guide-dog users exist in the world, passing able-bodied more than one would guess. It's why our stories matter so much in addressing bias, judgments, and assumptions when there is no cookie-cutter mold to disability and various aids to be more mobile and autonomous.

In our leadership, we have these same opportunities to advocate for the less obvious demographics, user experiences, and transcendent experiences we share that make us all worthy of dignity and being human. It's been an unexpected side quest than what I could even fathom when I was told the symptoms were permanent.

It's so important to use our influence to bridge what unites us. To show that being an asset to a team, having a seat at the table, and a baseline to build from make corporate culture and community better because of us. Not because of tokenism and tax credits.

Being vision impaired has shown me the power of creating even greater intentional visibility as a DEIA darling and inspiring others to see everyday opportunities to be a champion ambassador for a legacy-driven brand, already making an amazing impact in the world. Still, it can now have the opportunity to be aware of how accessibility and a more inclusive framework would break the invisible walls between able-bodied and the rest of the spectrum of the population that intersects from there.

How can we approach this conversation more in our leadership?

I believe it starts with creating opportunities to have these town hall conversations to have real feedback. Start to actively support vision-impaired creators, brands that support people with disabilities, and corporate structures that are modeling it well. Have a clear temperature check on your digital accessibility and intentionally seek out the local programs and organizations that serve these populations where you can find more knowledge and opportunities to bridge gaps in your backyard.

Being partially sighted has created a domino effect of questioning what's possible and even my bias and ignorance about blindness. Like most creative folks, I had learned to base my value on what I could create and do for others. Everything I perceived that made me valuable was based on what I could see.

My sense of autonomy, attention to detail, artistic talent, and so many services that required a lot of sensory input and dynamics to navigate are now more triggering. I went through a process of fighting for my sense of value to be more than what I could see or my capacity for how much I'm giving to the gift of understanding I create more impact and awareness with less than when I was wasting time and energy driving on those California highways. I now have a greater perspective to see through my other senses and intuition for creating safety and support with a different incubator experience.

The art of advocacy has never been more important.

How to implement more inclusion starts with knowing the basic pallet of DEIA

Every artist needs to have a handful of tools and knowledge base to get started with their landscape, and it's no different with the art and strategy behind a fully functioning DEIA landscape for a community, culture, client, or customer. For your initial pallet, you'll need to understand the primary prism that composes a diverse, rich canvas.

The primer for your canvass starts with how accessible your assets are for blind, low-vision, or people with disabilities for front-facing awareness of your service or product.

Next, depending on whether your business hires more talent in the future, you'll want to consider your complimentary color wheels for creative talent, assessing what changes may be needed to accommodate their success and how more inclusive experiences can shape the internal culture and decision making beyond simply checking a box.

The power of having a champion advocate as your set of brushes will ensure the right resources, programs, specific professionals, and engagement can ebb and flow on your canvass.

Every artist also knows there needs to be constructive criticism with their work to know how to improve a technique, create more depth or highlight; see where more practice needs to be invested, and ultimately continue mastering their craft. Does your corporate culture embrace feedback? Is your marketing accessible to those needing it from a web dev perspective? Is your team all on the same page about making changes and having room for more as needs arise?

An artist is trained to also be an advocate. In more policed parts of the world where communication and exposure are much more limited; art became a political voice to protest, bring awareness, speak on behalf of various demographics, push back on extreme injustice, and provide more confidence and expression, perspective, and color.

Are we, as leaders, willing to embrace the challenge of standing up against systemic policies, geographical discrimination, and a body of work that may require us to face disagreement and take a stronger stance that could personally affect our own security to support and ally with others? Sometimes, that is what the final reveal looks like in the gallery. A collection of triumphs, losses, chapters, seasons, and evolutions to reveal the growth and humanity that affects us all.

The art of advocacy truly becomes the art of awareness when we begin to understand the language, voice, and visibility our efforts bring daily and anchor into the progression where change will not be as immediate. Diversity becomes more about dignity, equity more about experience, inclusion more about impact, and accessibility more about awareness. That is our highest call to be an artist in our legacy-driven companies, our leadership teams, the boards we sit on, and our communities.

What landscape are you painting? Are you attached to how things are, or are you open to returning to the drawing board if things aren't working?

Real change happens because those in positions to create or decide on that change are already on board with it, not because they need to be convinced when there is resistance to the change that often requires more time, money, and manpower to address it if it can be changed.

We are all worthy of dignity and respect and finding a way to bridge what helps our creative and unique populations with the resources, opportunities, tools, and tech to thrive. The challenge is that most aren't thinking about the limitations one experiences when one can't access something they need, which able-bodied people may blatantly ignore or genuinely not even think is an issue until brought to their intention.

The power of being a champion lies so much in the heart to advocate for doing what is right and necessary, even if there is pushback, budgets don't have space, or decision-makers aren't receptive to the humanity in the conversation but will embrace it sheerly for their bottom line.

Being a champion is a badge of honor, no matter what stage of leadership you are in. There are opportunities to break barriers in your backyard or the business world, whether internally or externally.

Because of my lived experience, I've understood more system-ically the barriers and biases this gap between worlds faces. Through this community, I've discovered that my heart for advocacy and ambassadorship could soar in the accessibility and inclusion niche; I could bring dignity, visibility, and a voice to many who don't have access or awareness of opportunities to become our economy's greatest asset.

I've come to know that I have a unique way of seeing the world and people in a way that transcends color, race, and gender and finds the common denominator for those who need it the most.

While customer advocacy is not new regarding business strategy, retention, grassroots town halls, and corporate culture, it can be overlooked as an opportunity to serve a fuller spectrum of people, especially regarding accessibility and inclusion.

As I work with legacy-driven CEOs who often want to include an advocacy lens into the business plan, I've had opportunities to observe various approaches to the conversation and my own experience as part of the blind, low-vision, and people with disabilities community. Sometimes, our creative talent is brought on for business incentives, but not necessarily because a company wants to engage their standards and whether their talent can be set up to win.

Creativity and change sound wonderful and progressive in a creator economy that prides itself on creating more access. However, some people fall through the cracks simply because the marketing systems, user experiences, and avatars were not built with diversity in mind. Or the solutions become siloed in a sea of supposed inclusion, but there are divisions between each other.

So, how can we be better at being a champion that brings more voice and visibility here? How can we boy through bias and breakdowns?

We can start by taking a closer look at how DEIA leadership can access and embrace the conversation and then build from there regarding the internal or external influence we can bring as an ally. There is a framework to consider every opportunity for partnership or profit and would broaden the margin if companies understood the barriers existed.

With empathy, education, and greater engagement, I believe we can create more progress together for a world in which we all feel accepted and belong. This is the frame we can proudly showcase our portraits for the world to see. As you consider this chapter and the rest of the themes in this book, I encourage you to expose yourself to the thought leaders and opportunities to grow in inclusivity. Inquire about the best training and certifications you can find to create more accessibility. Allow yourself to be open to feedback on bottlenecks and barriers. Embrace the gifts and the gold you find along the way to understand the terms and language of acceptance.

As a final note to you and your current or inspired leadership journey: you are a leader with a visible or invisible challenge, and you may not always feel safe or respected in your current circle of influence to shine with. I implore that you are more than your diagnosis or disability. You have a seat in this conversation and a canvas waiting for your color choices, highlights, contests, detail, and valuable perspective. Be courageous enough to seek support groups and peer programs to explore more tools and spaces to have your voice heard. Embrace the powerful and unique ways your skill sets transfer in your palette and complement all that makes you a whole person. May these chapters blend more ambition over ambiguity and a body of work you will be proud of.

About the Author

Jessica is a strategic partnership consultant with Joyful Development Group. Legacy-driven brands work with her to discover, develop, and design their business development portfolios with ideal partnership matches. She is an advocacy artist, blues dance enthusiast, and makes a pretty mean shepherd's pie. For inquiries on how to amplify your impact and influence through strategic introductions, you can find her on LI, FB, and IG.

THE IMPACT OF INCLUSION AND ACCESSIBILITY ON CORPORATE SUCCESS AND CULTURE

DR. BRUCE RIPPEE

T he basic definition of inclusion involves equal access to opportunities and resources. On the surface, this seems like a good thing, and indeed, there are aspects of the social norm that require this to ensure an appropriate level of freedom, rights, and privileges. Fully understanding inclusion and accessibility requires more definition and nuance, or else, it seems, the two sides of the argument face off in exclusion and name-calling. I'm a firm believer in inclusion for equal opportunity, testing, and education, and I even allow for bias in outcomes based on loyalty, convenience, and a willingness to take responsibility.

Inclusion and accessibility are critical in the workplace for testing based on merits, abilities, and efforts. One of my favorite stories is about Junior, whom I met at the GM plant in Kansas City, Missouri. Junior was a 66-year-old black veteran who had been wounded in the line of duty. He walked with a limp and carried a mop bucket everywhere he went. We waved to each other a few times in the hallway before I struck up a conversation with him. I complimented him on the cleanliness of the hallways and the restrooms on the second floor and asked him how long he had worked at GM. The floodgates opened, and he told me the following story.

To his mother's chagrin, Junior's name was given to him by his younger brother because their father had the same name. He dropped out of high school at age sixteen to work at a gas station until he could join the Army. He was on the Army janitorial staff for eight years and then spent the next seventeen years preparing special events and cleaning the event spaces with about twenty other men and women.

He loved his time in the Army until he fell off of a ladder while hanging lights on poles for an event. He broke both lower leg bones and shattered the bones in his right ankle. After several surgeries and eighteen months at a desk, he retired with a decent pension and left the military. His retirement lasted only two months because he was bored, so he limped out of the house, went to GM, and got a job as a janitor at their Kansas City factory. Sadly, his wife died a year later, and he had no children. His brother, with whom he is still very close, told him that God was with him and he'd find a way to do God's work in this world. With that, Junior threw himself into his work. His work associates at GM became his family, and he worked twelve hours a day, six days a week. He told me that they made him go home because they refused to put a bed in the maintenance room.

At that time, GM was working toward the point system that made up a form of EEOC' inclusion,' and they received one point for hiring a black person, one point for hiring a veteran, and one point for hiring a person with a disability. Every hour Junior worked was worth three points toward EEOC guidelines, and he was offered all of the hours that he wanted. When I met him, he had already worked at GM for almost twenty years. Later in our friendship, Junior confided in me about the incredible opportunity he had been given.

"Dr. Bruce, how much do you think I'll make in a year?" he asked. I told him I knew he worked six days a week, twelve hours a day, and I hoped working as hard as he did and being as kind and loving as he is that it was all of the money that he could ever need. He smiled and said, "The first eight hours a day are paid normally, and the remaining four hours are paid at time and a half. When I come back after lunch on Thursday, I'll have completed my forty-hour work week. Each additional hour, for sixteen hours, is paid at time and a half, and the remaining sixteen hours are paid at double the hourly rate."

I told him he was living the American dream, and I was amazed and impressed. Then he said, "I put three nieces and a nephew through all of college and bought them all a car when they graduated. Chances are, doc, I'll make more than you." I told him that GM was lucky to have him because he really was amazing. When I asked him about the EEOC point system providing an opportunity for others, he said, "Listen, I show up early, and I start late. I tell them that I feel blessed to be part of GM, and these people have become my family. Maybe

I got this opportunity because of some system, but I keep it because my daddy and the military taught me how to work."

Junior is an example of a system working properly. Onboarding should be an opportunity to demonstrate one's merits, skills, and willingness to work for a company. Leaders should look to integrate those who not only have the skills to do the job but also those who simply want to work–and then give them the opportunity to succeed. However, I believe that we need to abandon the hope that all people have the same ability, desire, and temperament to learn skills and work well with others. The fact is that a portion of our society doesn't want to put in the effort or isn't suited for certain tasks. As long as leaders strive to include all segments of the population in hiring, firing, disciplining, training, etc., society will continue to find a place for those who want to be part of something bigger than themselves in the corporate world. If corporations are forced to make concessions for those who do not want to work or who cause problems in some way, 'inclusion' can be very costly.

Inclusion and accessibility solve problems for the few of us who fit that situation, but these people can be very helpful because they offer different perspectives. Also, a corporate culture of including those who are less able in some ways allows other workers to rally around those employees and create new systems while becoming mentors. Our culture in my clinics is to ask our more capable and longer-standing employees if they are willing to break down certain tasks into their constituent parts so that someone who is less capable can complete them with some success. In this way, everyone benefits. The teacher/mentor learns the job better by teaching it, and the learning employee has the opportunity to grasp the job and prove themselves in the position. I have always advocated that we hire anyone who can do the job well, can convince me that they really want the job by knowing the vision and the mission of the clinic and can be trained to do all of the above. I've also advocated for firing people who can't do the job, refuse to adapt to the corporate culture or make life all about themselves as opposed to the patients that we serve—no matter how capable they may be.

My flagship clinic is busy, and we have two front desk staff and one cashier. I remember when one of our check-in front desk associates pierced her tongue with a large spike. Unfortunately, one of her main duties was to talk to patients (many of whom are elderly and hard of hearing) and to answer the phone. She became almost unintelligible when she had her tongue pierced. We began to get complaints from our patients, especially those who spoke with her on the phone, so I took her aside and asked her if it was possible to remove it during when hours. She said, 'no,' and left our employ almost immediately after that. I never understood handicapping yourself on purpose, but there are those who do that and then seem to dare me to say something about their choices. Now, in this case, I didn't fire her, but I would have if she had not left on her own. The people who think she was in the right and that I should have asked her to stay do not own a company that serves the elderly. She was a good employee, and the opportunity was there, but she chose to create a handicap that was inconsistent with their job.

I think it's good to be open and include anyone a leader believes can do a good job without disrupting the corporate environment. We can promote inclusion by building opportunity into our culture and recognizing those who go above and beyond to educate and encourage those who are less talented. As I said before, our employees who become mentors become the best employees we have ever had. Leaders can also praise those who have been included and pay them well for their efforts, loyalty, and willingness to learn. We certainly do.

Promoting inclusion and accessibility gives a company a competitive advantage by showing that it truly cares about those in the community. When a company has the resources and cultivates a culture of care and outreach, inclusion is an obvious action that shows generosity and kindness. It is also important to note that the amount of inclusion will depend upon the size of the company since it should never hinder the company to the point of loss.

The best way to make inclusion and accessibility a reality is to create a culture of servant leadership and mentoring among employees. One of the best ways to integrate a community member into a company is for leaders to set up set times to meet with them. In this way, we have separated the ideology of inclusion (you got this job because you are...) from the fellow employee working next to us. We shouldn't just randomly include people; we should care about those who are ready to move the company forward and then create a culture that encourages and develops them.

If for some reason you take advice from me, I would suggest that leadership focus on intentional employee development meetings every month. Make it part of your culture to encourage every single employee and publicly recognize those who are making an effort to work with everyone else– regardless of ability. Once an employee adapts to and becomes part of the company culture, they're a member of the company. They are your teammates, and you should do everything you can to help them become productive. Recognizing those who help other team members is by far the best way to recognize a culture of servant leadership that empowers those who will help and creates the goodwill a company needs to thrive.

I'd like to see inclusion and accessibility lean heavily on those who accept responsibility for their actions and have the willingness to learn and grow and become strategically important to the organization. I am not a fan of the current narrative of dividing society into groups and then comparing the hardships of those groups. I believe that this leads us down a dark and difficult path. I realize that, in business, we should all be judged on our merits, our willingness to learn, our loyalty, and the qualities that make us good employees. I also believe that we should all have the opportunity to prove our worth and our desire to be valuable to a company.

The opportunity for abuse in an inclusive system comes from people who narcissistically force others to accommodate them, even though they don't have a disability and just want to be recognized as different and/or who are demanding rights and privileges they don't deserve. People who intentionally exclude themselves, exhibit racist behavior, ridicule people who have different opinions than they do, or exhibit other behaviors that don't build trust and a good working environment don't want to be included. In my opinion, it is hard enough to start and run a successful business, and those who refuse to follow the corporate rules, culture, and bylaws fire themselves. Also, if they have not followed the employee manual, they should certainly not be allowed any restitution from the business. Nearly seventy percent of all businesses fail in the first five years, and that is in an environment that is not burdened by the current social climate.

How can you create a culture of encouragement, praise, engagement, and mission that supports inclusion and accessibility? If you're asking to be included, be willing to take on the tasks asked of you to the best of your ability, so your inclusion strategically benefits morale, the bottom line, and the culture of the workplace. Every business needs and wants a Junior, and when we find one, we pay them well, publicly recognize their efforts, and ask them to mentor new employees.

About the Author

Dr. Bruce Rippee is a sought-after speaker, author, supplement formulator, and business development specialist. He spent the last thirty-one years researching and developing techniques that optimize how we sleep, think, eat, and move. His favorite patient is one who asks, "What can I do for myself?"

THE POWER OF EMPATHY AND ACCOMMODATION IN THE WORKPLACE

LUBA SAKHARUK

I magine a world where everyone has a fair chance to succeed. That's the world we want to build, and that's what the three books in this series are all about. These books are a treasure trove of wisdom on the important topics of leadership, diversity, equity, and inclusion. Each book addresses a different aspect of these topics, but they all have one common denominator: accessibility.

The first book on leadership and diversity shows us why diversity and inclusion are critical to success. Leaders who embrace diversity help their companies stay competitive, and they can deliver better results for their customers. The second book looks at the critical importance of equality and shows leaders how to be intentional about hiring. We can't just shrug our shoulders and say there aren't enough diverse applicants. We need to actively seek opportunities to connect with people outside our immediate network and challenge the status quo.

But what about accessibility? Until a few years ago, most of us probably only thought of accessibility in terms of wheelchair access. But in today's digital age, accessibility means so much more. When I started working for a company that provided online content through a learning management system, I quickly realized that accessibility was about much more than disabilities. We needed to create content that could be used by people with different learning styles and life situations. So we had to think about different personas and create content that was accessible on mobile devices.

To understand the true meaning of accessibility, I turned to a real expert: Ella Epshteyn. As someone who has led several accessibility projects in higher education, she knows what it takes to create truly accessible content. For Ella Epshteyn, accessibility and universal design concepts are at the heart of her work as CEO of ATTECS, a Boston-based company that provides instructional design and educational technology services.

Together, these books are an indispensable resource for all leaders who want to create a more inclusive, equitable, and accessible world.

"The first thing that comes to mind when we talk about accessibility is for the wider range of people from different walks of life, of different abilities to take advantage of the opportunities that society offers, whether it is shopping, entertainment or employment. Whether it services or goods or whatever, they should be able to have access to those. Accessibility is not about serving everyone. Because no matter how accessible we make goods and services, there is going to be a subset of population who is just not able to access. When we talk about accessibility, another important term is universal design. Universal design is about making goods and services accessible proactively. So not to accommodate someone who needs specific access, but to make sure that we design good services and pretty much everyday life in a way that it is accessible to as many people as possible. Inclusion is a little different."

Ella continued to share that accessibility started as a term to allow people with disabilities to access goods and services. But then we realized that when we make things accessible to people with disabilities, like those who have visual impairments or auditory impairments or any impairments, we're also making the same platforms, goods and services accessible to people who don't have disabilities, people that could get by, but it makes their life a lot easier.

"That includes people who, let's say, have spouses who are sleeping next to them, and they have to get up early, but they need to view some kind of training. Because the training is closed caption, now they can view that training without disturbing their spouse. People who don't have a good quiet environment for set training can go to the library and even though it's a quiet space, they can use that close captioning to access it."

When it comes to employment, accessibility is all about leveling the playing field and unleashing hidden talent. By ensuring that as many people as possible have access, organizations can tap into a larger pool of talent and bring in diverse perspectives. But what motivates organizations to prioritize accessibility?

In higher education, federal funding is a strong motivator. Institutions that receive federal funding must show that they're accessible or risk losing those funds. But for businesses, the motivators may be different. As Ella put it, they don't have the "whip" of federal funding forcing them to be more accessible.

So how can we get businesses to commit to accessibility? One approach is to link accessibility with innovation and competitiveness. When companies prioritize accessibility, they have access to a larger pool of talent, which can lead to more innovation and competitiveness. By connecting accessibility to these tangible benefits, we can motivate leaders to prioritize accessibility and create a more inclusive and accessible world.

Richa Bansal, Founder, and Managing Director of Saarathee (company who mission is to transform Persons with Disabilities (PwDs) into Professionals with Disabilities), runs an organization that truly believes in the concept of equitable opportunities. They offer jobs to largely PwDs (Persons with Disabilities) and promote employment of diverse disability groups. "Accessibility and Inclusion sit at the core of driving such equitable opportunities. I have seen a lot of companies comprehend accessibility to be only limited to mobility accessibility. However, the need to look at accessibility beyond that is crucial to include people with other forms of disabilities as well. I still feel that many corporations today stand unaware of limitations and the potential of certain disabled groups like the blind and people with learning disabilities – and they are equally unaware of how technology has become a great leveler. In the last five years, we have worked with over 500 PwD, and close to 70% of these have been people with vision impairment who have worked in fairly complex and challenging roles. Providing accessibility in the form of digital and physical has enabled them to perform at par or even better than the rest."

The story of Saarathee is truly inspirational,

"A few years ago, I chanced upon an opportunity to engage with people who could not see... and because of my limited understanding in the area... I thought that there isn't much I can expect from them... not being able to see is such a big handicap...Till these people turned my perception around... and for good. This was a group of highly passionate and motivated persons with visual impairment who were hired as tele-sales executives to drive sales targets for Vodafone; and a pilot of 3 months turned out to be a sustainable business proposition. My learning therefore was, that skills required to do a job can be tailored to suit a person with disabilities...So what if he can't see - he can talk, analyze, counsel, and lead, and do a whole lot more than any typical person can imagine... This insight and understanding then, became my purpose... This then became what we now call Saarathee."
–Richa Bansal, Founder

Organizations can embrace inclusion and accessibility by:

- Promoting mentorship and upskilling programs
- Allocating budget for certifications, trainings, and conferences
- Bringing in speakers and subject matter experts
- Organizing Lunch and Learn sessions to promote learning
- Organizing forums where employees can show off their expertise
- Sponsoring leadership program and focused offsites
- Emphasizing the importance of leaders empowering teams, growing people and leading with empathy!

In today's rapidly changing world, diversity, inclusion and accessibility have become increasingly important to businesses and organizations of all kinds. Not only do these values help create a more equitable society, but they can also lead to greater innovation, competitiveness and success.

But how can we ensure that we're truly living these values and not just paying lip service? One important factor is understanding the reasons behind our decisions. It's not enough to say we're committed to diversity and inclusion; we also need to understand the tangible benefits and outcomes these values can bring.

One important reason to prioritize diversity and inclusion is that it can help companies tap into a larger pool of talent. By creating a workplace culture that values diversity and welcomes people from all backgrounds, we can attract and keep top talent from a variety of populations. This can lead to greater creativity, innovation and productivity as team members bring unique perspectives and ideas to the table.

But creating a diverse and inclusive workplace isn't just about hiring a certain number of people from different backgrounds - it's about creating a culture that truly values and prioritizes diversity. That means actively seeking diverse perspectives, listening to the voices of marginalized groups and making them heard, and creating opportunities for people from different backgrounds to succeed.

One effective way to create an inclusive and accessible workplace is through training. By sharing our knowledge and experience, we can empower others to advance in their careers and take advantage of new opportunities. This is especially important for people from marginalized or underrepresented groups who face additional barriers.

But continuing education isn't just about helping others - it's also an opportunity for personal and professional growth. When we share our knowledge and experience with others, we can deepen our own understanding of our field and learn from the perspectives of others. This can help us become better leaders and team members, and can lead to greater success and satisfaction in our careers.

A good example of the power of continuing education is the Lead and Empower Her She Talks conferences organized by Dr. Julie Ducharme. These events bring women from around the world together to share stories, connect, and empower each other. By making these events accessible and affordable for women veterans, we can support those who have served our country and ensure that all have the opportunity to advance in their careers.

Inclusion and accessibility are about much more than just "checking off the boxes." It's about creating a workplace where everyone succeeds, regardless of their background or circumstances. By prioritizing education, knowledge sharing and creating meaningful connections, we can create a more diverse, inclusive and supportive world.

Of course, creating a more inclusive and accessible world is no easy task. It requires ongoing education, self-reflection, and a willingness to do the hard work of dismantling systems of oppression and inequality. But by working together, sharing our knowledge and experience, and making ourselves accessible to others, we can make real progress toward a more equitable society.

It's no secret that people are happier and more productive when they're treated with respect and understanding of their unique circumstances. As a leader, it's important to understand the importance of inclusion and accessibility in the workplace. I realized this during one of my recent assignments when I noticed that one employee never came into the office and didn't turn on his camera during meetings. After a few months, I learned he could not leave his home for health reasons but could still take part in every meeting via phone. Their expertise was invaluable, and they didn't want to be on disability. They wanted to work and had a lot of knowledge to share. This was a testament to the work culture because the company was understanding and responsive to their special needs.

It's important to recognize that accessibility isn't about accommodating everyone but about being inclusive and accommodating as much as possible. As leaders, we need to be aware of our employees' unique circumstances and proactively create workplaces that are diverse, equitable, inclusive, and accessible. When employees feel cared for and included, they're more engaged and productive, leading to greater success for the organization.

Inclusion and accessibility in the workplace also give companies access to a broader range of talent, making them more competitive. When companies emphasize inclusion and accessibility, they open the doors to people who might otherwise be excluded. This leads to more innovation and creativity as different perspectives are brought in. In a rapidly changing world, a diverse and talented team can give companies the competitive edge they need to succeed.

It's important to know that treating people with respect and understanding isn't only good for business, it's the right thing to do. A few years ago, I had to work in another country for weeks at a time for family reasons. My company was incredibly understanding and accommodating and allowed me to access everything I needed to get my work done. This not only allowed me to fulfill my obligations to my family but also to my team members, who had access to me despite the physical distance. When you take care of your employees, they feel valued and appreciated, which leads to greater loyalty and retention.

At the end of the day, it's about people. When we focus on the well-being of our employees, we create a culture of respect and understanding that leads to greater success for everyone involved. Leaders who are intentional, deliberate, and proactive in creating diverse, equitable, inclusive, and accessible workplaces are better positioned to thrive in today's rapidly changing world.

ABOUT THE AUTHOR

Luba Sakharuk holds a master's degree in computer science from Worcester Polytech Institute of Technology and started her career as a software engineer. The unique insights and abilities she gained in her career led her to agile coaching, facilitation, training, leadership, and digital transformations. While working full time as a senior lead consultant, she published two books and founded RALM3 Consulting LLC, focusing on public speaking, facilitation, and mentorship.

Empowering Your Team Through Inclusion and Accessibility

David Wolf

At the heart of any successful business is the value of inclusion. It's not just about making everyone feel welcome, but about each individual bringing unique skills and perspectives that benefit the company. This means embracing diversity in all its forms and creating a culture where everyone feels valued and heard.

But it's not just about the people within the company. Accessibility is just as important. It's about making sure that the work being done is accessible to everyone, whether it's a customer looking to buy a product or an employee looking to contribute to a project. That means breaking down barriers and creating an environment where everyone has an equal opportunity to participate and succeed.

So if you want to build a truly inclusive and accessible company, it starts with a mindset that values diversity and recognizes the unique contributions everyone can make. If you create a culture that takes these principles to heart, you'll not only attract the best talent, but you'll also build a loyal customer base that feels seen, heard, and valued.

At Audivita, inclusion and accessibility aren't just buzzwords, they're at the core of who we are as a company. It's an essential part of our DNA. That's why we've carefully assembled a team of people who share these values and bring them to life in everything we do. We're proud of our DNA and excited to share it with you.

We believe everyone should have the opportunity to contribute. That's why we work tirelessly to ensure our products are accessible to everyone, regardless of their skills or background. It's about meeting a minimum standard and striving to go above and beyond to create products that are inclusive and welcoming to all.

As a leader, I believe values are a way of life. That's why I strive to embody the values of inclusion and accessibility in everything I do. I know my team looks to me for guidance, and I take that responsibility seriously.

But it's not just about me; it's about all of us. Every one of us can make a difference and create a culture that values diversity and promotes inclusion. I encourage everyone on my team to bring their unique perspectives and ideas to the table and work together to develop services that are accessible to all.

We have learned that an ounce of prevention is worth more than a pound of cure. By creating a culture of inclusion and accessibility from the beginning, we have been able to avoid many of the conflicts and tensions that can plague a workplace. This has allowed us to be more productive and create a more equitable environment for all.

While we haven't encountered specific problems that can be solved only with inclusion and accessibility, we believe these values are essential for any company that wants to succeed in today's world. By valuing diversity and creating an environment where everyone feels valued, we can realize the full potential of our team and develop products that truly meet our customers' needs.

So if you want to create a more productive and harmonious workplace, consider the values of inclusion and accessibility. They may not solve all your problems, but they'll certainly put you on the path to success.

At the end of the day, words are just words. To truly promote the values of inclusion and accessibility, you must lead by example. As a manager or leader, your actions say more than any mission statement or company policy. By living our values every day, we create a culture that values diversity and encourages everyone to contribute their unique perspectives and ideas.

If you want to promote the values of inclusion and accessibility in your company, start by looking in the mirror. Are you really living these values, or are they just empty words on a piece of paper? When you embody these values in your actions, you create a culture that truly values diversity and inclusion, and that's a recipe for success.

Building a successful brand is about your core values. Your brand reflects who you're and what you believe in, and it's that authentic expression that truly sets you apart in a crowded marketplace.

Best of all, this approach isn't just good for our brand, but it's good for our bottom line. By creating a culture that values diversity and inclusion, we attract the best talent and build a loyal customer base that shares our vision for a better world. It creates a situation that sets in motion a powerful, regenerative spiral of success.

To build a brand that really stands out in a crowded marketplace, focus on your core values. By embodying those values in everything you do, you'll create a brand that's not only competitive but also has great meaning for your customers and team members.

ABOUT THE AUTHOR

David Wolf is a seasoned music composer and audio content producer for various media platforms, with experience working for notable studios and brands through his previous company, Crywolf Productions, Inc. He founded Audivita Studios to leverage his expertise and his creative team's talents in assisting businesses, influencers, and thought leaders in growing their brands through podcasting, audiobooks, video, and internet radio. His extensive client list includes industry giants such as NBC Universal, Disney, Procter & Gamble, and Southwest Airlines.

Dear Entrepreneur,

Are you looking for a way to take your business to the next level? Writing a co-authored book could be the answer you've been searching for.

As an entrepreneur, you know the importance of building an authoritative presence in your industry. When you co-author a book, it adds instant credibility to your name and opens the door to increased influence and networking opportunities.

That's why SAB Publishing is excited to offer you this unique opportunity. Co-authoring a book with us gives you the chance to become a bestselling author and increase your lead flow. Plus, you'll be able to build your brand and grow your business.

At SAB Publishing, we understand the needs of entrepreneurs like you. That's why we make it easy to write a co-authored book with us. An experienced publisher and editor helps you write a compelling story, as well as professional design and marketing services.

Take the first step to becoming a bestselling author and growing your business.

Contact SAB Publishing today (jetlaunch.link/sp) to learn more about our co-authoring opportunities to grow your business.

Chris O'Byrne
SAB Publishing
books@strategicadvisorboard.com

SAB
PUBLISHING

www.ingramcontent.com/pod-product-compliance
Lightning Source LLC
Chambersburg PA
CBHW031400180326
41458CB00043B/6550/J